SOLENT
REVIEW 2005

F233

Photograph Credits

In addition to the many International Navies and Organisations who kindly forwarded images many of the stunning photographs used in this guide have been taken by private photographers who regularly contribute to *Warship World* magazine. We regret we are unable to supply copies as most are private individuals rather than commercial photographers.

Our thanks go to, Gary Davies, Nick Newns, David Hannaford, Stuart Miller, Dave Cullen, Dane Murdoch, Chris Rogers, Derek Fox, Walter Sartori, Daniel Ferro, Neill Rush and Michael Nitz for their continuing support

To contact Maritime Photographic visit:
www.maritimephotographic.co.uk

Published by Maritime Books, Lodge Hill, Liskeard, Cornwall PL14 4EL, England

Introduction

It is an honour to be asked to introduce this short brochure on the Fleet Review on the occasion of the 200th anniversary of Nelson's great victory at Trafalgar. In the past centuries, our enemies of that time have become our close friends and allies, and it is to celebrate that friendship that so many nations are participating in this most historic occasion.

Although the Fleet has been reviewed by the Sovereign since 1415, when Henry V inspected his invasion force which took his army eventually to the battle of Agincourt, they are relatively rare events: fewer than 50 have been held in the past 600 years, most of these at Spithead, off Portsmouth. Today is therefore a special day, to be held in the memory for a long time.

Originally, Fleet Reviews were held either to mobilize the Fleet for war, or as a warning to potential enemies on the power of the Royal Navy. Now, in these happy times of relative peace, the purpose of the Review is in commemoration of a key anniversary in the national calendar, or the expression of gratitude for a Royal Jubilee, and we take great pride and pleasure in inviting the ships of other navies to join in our celebrations.

In these days of internet commerce and airline travel, it is sometimes easy to forget that the trading system of the world is still almost completely dependent on the sea and in the will of nations to preserve and police that system, in the last resort, by seapower. The ships anchored for this review off Portsmouth are a living testimony that there are still many countries that understand the value of navies and the enduring lessons of history.

Captain Christopher Page Royal Navy (Retired)
Head of the Naval Historical Branch of the Ministry of Defence
June 2005

SHIPS OF THE
ROYAL NAVY & ROYAL FLEET AUXILIARY
ATTENDING THE FLEET REVIEW 2005

Aircraft Carriers

INVINCIBLE	R05
ILLUSTRIOUS	R06

Destroyers

EXETER	D89
SOUTHAMPTON	D90
NOTTINGHAM	D91
MANCHESTER	D95
GLOUCESTER	D96
CARDIFF	D108

Frigates

GRAFTON	F80
SUTHERLAND	F81
ST ALBANS	F83
CUMBERLAND	F85
CHATHAM	F87
LANCASTER	F229
MARLBOROUGH	F233
IRON DUKE	F234
MONMOUTH	F235
MONTROSE	F236
WESTMINSTER	F237

Submarines

TRAFALGAR
SOVEREIGN
TURBULENT

Assault Ships

OCEAN	L12
ALBION	L14

BULWARK	L15

Minehunters

BRECON	M29
LEDBURY	M30
CATTISTOCK	M31
COTTESMORE	M32
MIDDLETON	M34
DULVERTON	M35
CHIDDINGFOLD	M37
WALNEY	M104
PEMBROKE	M107
GRIMSBY	M108
BANGOR	M109
RAMSEY	M110
SHOREHAM	M112

Patrol Craft

EXPLORER	P164
EXAMPLE	P165
LEEDS CASTLE	P258
ARCHER	P264
TRACKER	P274
RAIDER	P275
BLAZER	P279
TYNE	P281
PUNCHER	P291
RANGER	P293
TRUMPETER	P294

Survey Ships

GLEANER	H86
ENTERPRISE	H88
ROEBUCK	H130
SCOTT	H131

ENDURANCE	A171

SIR TRISTRAM	L3505

Royal Fleet Auxiliaries

Strategic Sealift Ro-Ro Ferry

ORANGELEAF	A110
ARGUS	A135
FORT VICTORIA	A387
FORT GEORGE	A388
WAVE RULER	A390
SIR BEDIVERE	L3004
SIR GALAHAD	L3005

MV HURST POINT

Royal Logistic Corps

RLCV AACHEN	L110
RLCV AREZZO	L111
RLCV AUDEMER	L113

NAVAL GLOSSARY

Navies worldwide use a lot of abbreviations and jargon, some of which have crept into this guide. Here are a few to help you out.

AEW	Airborne Early Warning
ASW	Anti-Submarine Warfare
ASROC	Anti-Submarine Rocket. US Missile System.
CIWS	Close In Weapon System
CODAG	Combined Diesel and Gas
CODLAG	Combined Diesel Electric and Gas
COGAG	Combined Gas and Gas
COGOG	Combined Gas or Gas
GPMG	General Purpose Machine Gun
LCU	Landing Carft Utility
MCM	Mine Countermeasures
MCMV	Mine Countermeasures Vessel
NATO	North Atlantic Treaty Organisation
RAM	Rolling Airframe Missile
RHIB	Rigid Hulled Inflatable Boat
RM	Royal Marines
ROV	Remotely Operated Vessel
SAM	Surface to Air Missile
SSN	Nuclear Powered Submarine
SSM	Surface to Surface Missile
VERTREP	Vertical Replenishment - Transferring stores between ships by helicopter
VL	Vertical Launch
VLS	Vertical Launch System
VSTOL	Vertical Short Take-off Or Landing

THE FLEET REVIEW PROGRAMME

The following are the highlights of the Fleet Review programme. Her Majesty the Queen will inspect warships from up to 40 navies present accompanied by an array of merchant and tall ships anchored in the Solent on 28th June. The full programme is as follows

24 -27 June: Ships anchor in the Solent - see enclosed anchorage plan on pages 8-9.

pm 27 June   Full Rehearsal

28 June

1 -3pm   Her Majesty inspects the Fleet. She will be onboard the Ice Patrol ship HMS Endurance (You won't miss her in her Red paintwork!)

3.15 - 4.30pm   Sail and Fly Past. Up to 86 aircraft from around the world are expected.

5.30 pm   Flying Display commences. Air Display includes: Red Arrows (5.30 - 5.50pm) Spitfire, Yakovlevs, Sukhoi Su-26, Army Blue Eagles Helicopter Display Team

Evening   Son et Lumiere. A magnificent Sound and Light display featuring an illustration of a 19th Century sea battle...This event will take place in the channel between Southsea Castle and Clarence Pier.

7pm   Show starts

8.15pm   Nelson rowed to his flagship (Grand Turk) from Southsea beach

9.40pm   Battle commences!

10.10pm   Firework display

10.30pm   The International Fleet are illuminated at anchor

29 June   INTERNATIONAL DRUMHEAD CEREMONY. All day. Many ships leave their anchorages in the Solent and sail into Portsmouth Naval base. (Details on Radio Solent 96.1 and 103.8 FM) Best seen from the area north of Clarence Pier.

11am   Private Drumhead Ceremony on Southsea Common for invited veterans.(includes Flypast by RN Historic Aircraft)

3pm - 8pm   Veterans centre open to the public on Southsea common. Royal Marine Band

30th June - 3rd July.

INTERNATIONAL FESTIVAL OF THE SEA in Portsmouth Naval Base. A four day festival packed with entertainment, spectacle and fun in a harbour packed with ships of all sizes. Your opportunity to visit warships, tall ships and yachts of all sizes from around the world. (Don't forget to come and see us in our exhibition trailer between HMS ILLUSTRIOUS and the Greek and Russian warships at the west end of Fountain lake jetty. See all our book bargains and souvenirs!)

OUR TIP FOR VISITORS TO THE AREA.

1) Leave your car at home (or use the park and ride facilities if you must use it to get to the area)

2) To get closest to the ships at the review go to Gosport (Stokes Bay or Gilkicker). Take the Train to Portsmouth Harbour and then the ferry and bus.

3) Listen to BBC Radio Solent on 96.1 or 103.8 or Navy Radio on 87.9 for all the latest news on the day.

4) Go back to Southsea in the evening for the Son et Lumiere and fireworks.

The above Information was correct as we closed for press (on 7th June)

With this Guide book and access to a Radio you'll have all the information you need to go to the Fleet Review.

BBC Radio Solent are broadcasting as follows on Tuesday 28th June

0700-0900	Breakfast Show, Solent Today, live overlooking the Solent.
Approx 1120-1220	Live reports covering H M The Queen's arrival in Portsmouth.
1230-1700	International Fleet Review programme,live from ships in the Solent and ashore too.
1730-1900	Live from Southsea Common - Air Display
1900-2300	Son et Lumiere programme live from Clarence Esplanade. Reporters on Southsea Common and on board Grand Turk.

TRAFFIC reports all day right through to 0100 Wednesday

All programmes will be broadcast on BBC Radio Solent 96.1FM (Hants, Dorset and Isle of Wight)and 103.8FM (West Dorset). The Son et Lumiere programme will also be broadcast on BBC locals radio stations across the south including Kent (96.7FM), Oxford (95.2FM), Berks 104.1FM), Southern Counties (104-104.8FM and 95.3FM).Listen if you have to go home early.

Radio Solent broadcast Shipping forecasts, which includes shipping movements, at 0535 and 0645 daily. Shipping movements are then repeated at 0845.

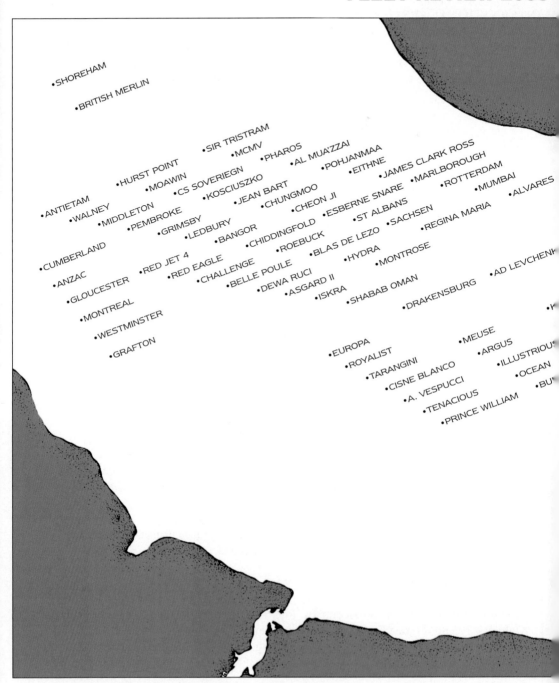

- SHOREHAM
- BRITISH MERLIN
- SIR TRISTRAM
- MCMV
- PHAROS
- AL MUA'ZZAI
- POHJANMAA
- HURST POINT
- EITHNE
- JAMES CLARK ROSS
- MARLBOROUGH
- ROTTERDAM
- MOAWIN
- CS SOVERIEGN
- KOSCIUSZKO
- MUMBAI
- ALVARES
- ANTIETAM
- MIDDLETON
- JEAN BART
- CHUNGMOO
- CHEON JI
- ESBERNE SNARE
- WALNEY
- PEMBROKE
- ST ALBANS
- SACHSEN
- GRIMSBY
- LEDBURY
- BANGOR
- CHIDDINGFOLD
- REGINA MARIA
- CUMBERLAND
- ROEBUCK
- BLAS DE LEZO
- MONTROSE
- ANZAC
- RED JET 4
- CHALLENGE
- HYDRA
- AD LEVCHENK
- GLOUCESTER
- RED EAGLE
- BELLE POULE
- DEWA RUCI
- ASGARD II
- SHABAB OMAN
- MONTREAL
- ISKRA
- DRAKENSBURG
- WESTMINSTER
- GRAFTON
- MEUSE
- EUROPA
- ARGUS
- ROYALIST
- ILLUSTRIOU
- TARANGINI
- CISNE BLANCO
- OCEAN
- A. VESPUCCI
- BU
- TENACIOUS
- PRINCE WILLIAM

In addition to those ships listed the following will be assigned to security patrols: HM Ships Manchester, Sutherland, Monmouth, Leeds Castle, Brecon, Cottesmore and Dulverton.

ANCHORAGE PLAN

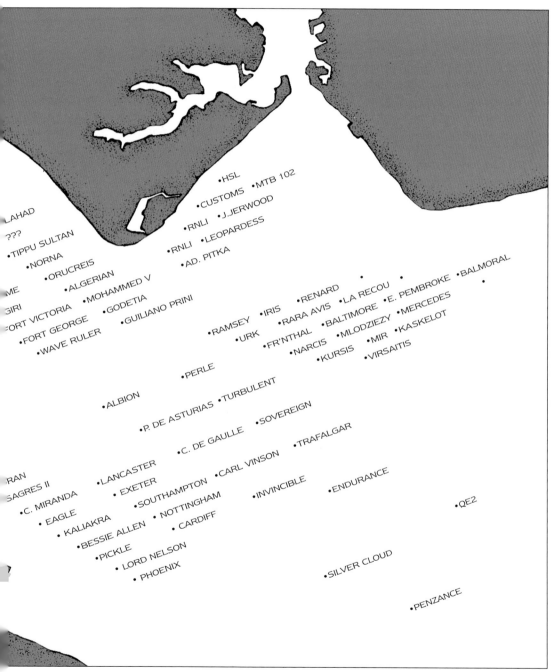

This chart was drawn up well before the review and it is likely that some ships will be in different anchor berths by the time the review takes place. Despite doing our level best, security measures prevented us getting you the very latest positions of ships - we can only apologise.

Author's Notes

It was a from a similar publication by Mike Critchley in 1977 that Maritime Books was born. The relative ease with which he produced a guide to the 1977 Silver Jubilee Review was the "trump card" in convincing me to produce a similar book for the Trafalgar 200 commemorations. With the encouraging words "a couple of hours cutting and pasting" ringing in my ears, I agreed to write this book. It turned out to be a whole lot more........

The effort required shows just how much the world has changed in the intervening 27 years. While a Fleet Assembly in the Solent is without doubt a spectacular sight for the public, foremost in the planners minds now is that such an assembly of international naval might is also a prime terrorist target. With this threat uppermost the organisers are careful to weigh the needs of security against the requests of authors. This has made the compilation of this book far from being the easy task that was sold to me!

That said, the support received from various organisations, Embassies, International Companies and Charities to make this come together has been superb and my thanks are due to them all.

Particular thanks must go to the team at the Trafalgar 200 office and in particular to Lt Francesca Woodman who has fielded a myriad of e-mails and calls with great patience and provided as much information as possible within the security constraints. Without her help this volume would have been very thin.

An event as large as an International Fleet Review is very fluid - ships pulling out at the last minute; others being replaced by substitutes and others not wishing their visit to be publicised in advance. I have tried to be as accurate as possible, but to meet the publication deadline stumps had to be drawn at some stage (7 June). If there are omissions or inacurracies I hope you will appreciate that such a guide book can only be as accurate as the information to hand at the time of publication. The book is not intended as an historical reference - rather a guide to give the public a little background on the ships in attendance and to enhance their experience of the spectacle.

There is a handy list by pennant number on the last two pages to help the reader identify the many ships on review. I trust that you take some great memories home with you.

Steve Bush
June 2005

HM Ships Invincible & Illustrious

MOD/CROWN COPYRIGHT

Aircraft Carriers

Invincible	**R05**
Illustrious	**R06**

Displacement:	22,000 tons
Dimensions:	210 x 36 x 6.5 m
Propulsion:	COGAG (Combined Gas and Gas); 2 shafts; 4 Rolls-Royce Olympus Gas Turbines.
Speed:	28 kts
Armament:	3 x Goalkeeper Close In Weapon System (CIWS); 2 x 20mm close range guns
Aircraft:	A mix of Harrier GR7/9; Sea King ASaC7; Merlin.
Complement:	685 Ship's Company 386 Air Group

Originally conceived in the 1980's as Anti-Submarine carriers during the cold war, the RN's three aircraft carriers have evolved into effective Strike carriers, able to deploy tailored Air Groups to support global operations, against a multitude of potential targets.

Illustrious has recently emerged from refit and is to assume the role of fleet flagship. Invincible will retire into reserve shortly and is unlikely to see further RN service before the introduction of two promised new large aircraft carriers into the RN. The third carrier Ark Royal, currently laid up, will enter refit in 2006 to eventually replace Invincible as a second operational aircraft carrier.

Helicopter Carrier (LPH)

Ocean	**L12**

Displacement:	22,000 tons
Dimensions:	203.4 x 32.6 x 6.65 m
Propulsion:	2 x Crossley-Pielstick diesels; two shafts and a bow thruster.
Speed:	18 kts
Aircraft:	12 x Sea King HC4; 6 x Lynx Can operate Chinook and Apache.
Armament:	3 x Phalanx CIWS; 2 x 20mm Close range guns.
Complement:	285 Ship's Company

HMS Ocean

HM Ships Albion & Bulwark

206 Aircrew
(Max 1275 with Royal
Marines embarked)

HMS Ocean was named by HM The Queen on 20 February 1998 at Barrow-in-Furness. She is the largest ship in the Royal Navy and the first purpose-built helicopter carrier, designed for the rapid landing of an assault force by air and sea. As the only one of her class and highly versatile platform, she is much in demand in today's strategic environment. She has a reputation for never finishing a deployment as planned; in 1998 whilst on trials she assisted in hurricane relief in Nicaragua, in 1999 she took part in the earthquake relief operation in Turkey and in 2000 she was diverted to Sierra Leone twice. In 2001, after 11 September, the ship returned to the UK to be made ready for continuing operations in the campaign against terrorism which resulted in her participation in Operation TELIC during the Iraq War. Since then she has taken part in Exercise Aurora in the United States and a Joint Maritime Course, proving her capability in littoral and amphibious operations. Now having gained a very satisfactory report at Basic Operational Sea Training she is preparing for Bowman radio trials and Amphibious training through the rest of 2005.

Assault Ship (LPD)

Albion	**L14**
Bulwark	**L15**

Displacement:	18,500 tons
	21,500 tons (ballasted)
Dimensions:	176 x 28.9 x 6.1 m
Propulsion:	Electric propulsion. 2 x 6.25Mw and 2 x 1.56Mw diesel generators driving two shafts and a bow thruster.
Speed:	18 kts
Aircraft:	Two spot 64 m flight deck capable of operating helicopters up to Chinook size.
Armament:	2 x Goalkeeper CIWS; 2 x 20mm close range guns
Complement:	325
	305 Troops (overload of a further 405)

HMS Albion arrived at Devonport on 3 April 2003 and commissioned on 19 June. After many delays at the builders HMS Bulwark, the Navy's newest ship, was handed over in July 2004 and became operational only last month. Their integral vehicle deck has a capacity for up to six Challenger 2 tanks or around 30 armoured all-terrain tracked vehicles. A floodable well dock, has the capacity to take four utility landing craft (each capable of carrying a Challenger 2 tank). Four smaller landing craft are on davits, each capable of carrying 35 troops. A two-spot flight deck is able to take medium support helicopters and stow a third. The Flight Deck is capable of taking the Chinook helicopter. Earlier financial savings means it does not have a hangar as planned but has all the equipment needed to support aircraft operations.

Nuclear Powered Submarines

Trafalgar	
Turbulent	

Displacement:	5,200 tons (Dived)
Dimensions:	85.4 x 9.8 x 9.5 m
Armament:	5 tubes capable of firing both Spearfish torpedoes or

HMS Trafalgar

DAVID HANNAFORD

13

STUART MILLER

HMS Nottingham

Tomahawk cruise missiles.

Complement: 130

Sovereign

Displacement: 4,900 tonnes (Dived)
Dimensions: 82.9 x 9.8 x 8.5 m
Armament: 5 tubes capable of firing
                Spearfish torpedoes
Complement: 116

Quiet, fast and with an almost unlimited endurance the nuclear-powered submarines of the Royal Navy are in the vanguard of many operations. Able to operate undetected they can conduct surveillance, undetake covert troop insertion, anti-ship, anti-submarine and land attack missions with virtual impunity.

Destroyers

Exeter	**D89**
Southampton	**D90**
Nottingham	**D91**
Cardiff	**D118**

Displacement: 4,820 tonnes
Dimensions: 125 x 14.3 m

Propulsion: COGOG (Combined Gas and
                Gas) 2 x Olympus and 2 x
                Tyne gas turbines; 2 shafts
Speed: 30 kts
Aircraft: Lynx
Armament: Twin Sea Dart Missile
                launcher; 4.5-inch gun; 2 x
                20mm close range guns; 2 x
                Phalanx CIWS; 2 x triple
                ASW torpedo tubes; Sea
                Gnat and DLF3 decoy
                launchers.
Complement: 287

Manchester	**D95**
Gloucester	**D96**

Displacement: 5,200 tonnes
Dimensions: 141 x 15.2 m
Propulsion: COGOG (Combined Gas and
                Gas) 2 x Olympus and 2 x
                Tyne gas turbines; 2 shafts
Speed: 30 kts
Aircraft: Lynx
Armament: Twin Sea Dart Missile
                launcher; 4.5-inch gun; 2 x
                20mm close range guns; 2 x
                Phalanx CIWS; 2 x triple
                ASW torpedo tubes; Sea

Gnat and DLF3 decoy launchers.

Complement: 287

Although near the end of their service lives the remaining Batch II Type 42 Destroyers and the younger Batch III ships still form the backbone of the Royal Navy's anti-air warfare capability. They are equipped with the Sea Dart medium range air defence missile system, which in its primary role is designed to provide area air defence for a group of ships, although it is also effective against surface targets at sea. The Type 42 Destroyers also operate independently carrying out patrol and boarding operations, recently enforcing UN embargoes in the Gulf and the Adriatic as well as providing humanitarian assistance in Monserrat and East Timor.

Frigates

Grafton	**F80**
Sutherland	**F81**
St Albans	**F83**
Lancaster	**F229**
Marlborough	**F233**
Iron Duke	**F234**
Monmouth	**F235**
Montrose	**F236**
Westminster	**F237**

Displacement:	4,900 tonnes
Dimensions:	133 x 16.1 m
Propulsion:	Turbines:CODLAG (Combined Diesel and Gas) 2 x Rolls-Royce Spey gas boost Diesels: 4 x GEC-Alsthom Paxman Valenta. Electric: 2 x GEC motors
Speed:	28 kts
Armament:	2 x Quad Harpoon Missile launchers; Vertical Launch Sea Wolf missiles; 4.5-inch Mk 8 gun; 2 x 30mm close range guns; 2 x Magazine launched ASW torpedo tubes; NATO Seagnat and DLF3 Decoy Launchers.
Aircraft:	Merlin or Lynx helicopter
Complement:	185

The 13 remaining Type 23 frigates are the most modern in the surface fleet, forming 50% of the total frigate/destroyer force in the Royal Navy. Originally designed for the principal task of anti-submarine warfare, they have evolved into

HMS St Albans

F83

DANE MURDOCH

DANIEL FERRO

powerful and versatile multi purpose ships with the capability to operate anywhere in the world. The ships were designed with stealth in mind, and the strangely angled superstructure reduces their radar signature significantly. The ships have in the past been tasked on embargo operations, disaster relief work and surveillance operations and counter drug operations.

Iron Duke

HMS Iron Duke is the third ship to bear the name and the fifth Type 23 Frigate to be built, being accepted into service on 23 July 1992. Commanded by Commander Andy Jordan, the-ship has spent the past 5 months conducting UK exercises involving submarines and other HM ships. She sailed from Devonport on the 24 June to take part in the Fleet Review, before returning back to Devonport to continue her Operational Sea Training.

Montrose

Commanded by Cdr Andrew Webb, this year has seen HMS Montrose sail on her first deployment for 2 years. Joining a Carrier led task group, she recently completed exercises in the Gulf. This was the first time an Aircraft

Carrier had operated east of Suez since the Gulf War. She participated in a Joint, Multi-National exercise off Oman as well as contributing to the global war on terror by carrying out Maritime Interdiction Operations in the region.

Following the Fleet Review the ship will embark on a busy summer programme with future Navigating Officers and Principle Warfare Officers putting their skills to the test around the south coast before summer leave and maintenance prior to deploying in the autumn.

St Albans

After completing a six and a half month overseas deployment HMS St Albans returned to the UK in May 2004.

The start of 2005 saw the ship undergo a highly intensive six week training programme off the South Coast. Every area and aspect of the ship was assessed, scrutinised and pushed to it's absolute limit. Thereafter this, the navy's newest Type 23 Frigate, proceeded to the North Sea to put it's training into practice during a Joint Maritime Course which brings together both the Royal Navy and other foreign Navies to train and work together in a 'realistic' environment.

After the Fleet Review the ship will take some well earned Summer Leave before starting preparations for a forthcoming deployment to the Gulf in February 2006.

Cumberland	**F85**
Chatham	**F87**

Displacement:	5,300 tonnes
Dimensions:	148.1 x 14.8 m
Propulsion:	COGAG; 2 x Rolls-Royce Spey gas turbines; 2 x Rolls-Royce Tyne gas turbines
Speed:	30+ kts
Aircraft:	Sea King or up to 2 Lynx
Armament:	4.5-inch Mk 8 gun; Goalkeeper CIWS; Sea Wolf missile system; 2 x Quad Harpoon missile launchers; 2 x 20mm close range guns; NATO Seagnat Decoy Launchers.
Complement:	250 (Max 301)

Originally designed as specialist anti-submarine vessels, the Type 22 Frigates have evolved into a powerful surface combatant with substantial anti-surface, anti-submarine and anti aircraft weapons systems. They also possesses excellent command & control and communication facilities, making them ideal Flagships for senior officers. On patrol they have an efficient cruising speed of 18 knots, but have a sprint capability of over 30 knots.

Minehunters

Brecon	**M29**
Ledbury	**M30**
Cattistock	**M31**
Cottesmore	**M32**
Middleton	**M34**
Dulverton	**M35**
Chiddingfold	**M37**

Displacement:	750 tonnes
Dimensions:	60 x 10.5 m
Propulsion:	2 x Ruston-Paxman Deltic 9-58K diesels developing 1900hp; 1 Deltic 9-59 diesel for pulse generation and auxiliary drive; 2 shafts and a bow thruster.
Speed:	15 kts
Armament:	1 x 30mm; 2 x BMarc 20mm;

HMS Ledbury

M30

HMS Grimsby

| | 2 x General Purpose Machine Guns. |
| Complement: | 45 |

The Hunt Class are the largest warships ever constructed out of Glass Reinforced Plastic. These ships are able to both hunt and sweep mines. They can destroy buoyant mines by cutting the mooring wires with a towed wire sweep and then blowing up the buoyant case on the surface. Ground mines (weapons that sit on the sea bed listening for ship's noise and magnetic signatures) are swept using influence sweeps which simulate noise and magnetic signature. In the Minehunter role they employ high definition sonar to locate any mine and then destroy them using explosives placed either by the ships Mine Clearance Divers or by the Remote Controlled Mine Disposal System Vehicles. In addition, the 1 x 30mm, 2 x 20mm guns and two General Purpose Machine Guns (GPMGs) enable them to function in a Secondary Role as very potent patrol Craft. The Hunt class are often found supporting the Fishery Protection Squadron around UK waters.

Cattistock

HMS Cattistock completed a refit in April 2004

at Rosyth and spent the latter part of 2004 and early 2005 conducting trials and Operational Sea Training designed to raise the Ship to the high level operational standard required to conduct live operations.

In April 2005 the ship sailed from Portsmouth for a three month deployment to the Baltic to participate in multinational exercises with other NATO and Baltic Navies. These included the NATO Exercise Loyal Mariner, Polish MCM Squadex and the US Sponsored BALTOPS. In addition to this the Ship participated in live operations off Lithuania clearing World War 2 and Cold War minefields and abandoned ordnance. During the deployment Cattistock visited Frederikshavn and Copenhagen in Denmark, Gdynia in Poland, Karlskrona in Sweden, Klaipeda in Lithuania, Liepaja in Latvia and Kiel in Germany before returning to the UK via the Kiel canal.

Following the Fleet Review the Ship will visit Poole to renew her affiliation with Cattistock Village and then return to Portsmouth for a period of maintenance and Leave before taking on fishery protection duties at the end of the year.

Walney	**M104**
Pembroke	**M107**
Grimsby	**M108**

Bangor	**M109**
Ramsey	**M110**
Shoreham	**M112**

Displacement:	600 tonnes
Dimensions:	52.5 x 10.9 m
Propulsion:	2 x Paxman Valenta diesels;
	Voith-Schnieder propulsion;
	2 x Schottel bow thrusters
Speed:	13 kts
Armament:	1 x 30 mm gun
Complement:	34 (Max 40)

By comparison to the earlier Hunt class, the eight ships of the Sandown class are specialist Minehunters, being equipped with sonar and submersibles to hunt out mines.

Grimsby

HMS Grimsby is part of MCM 1 Squadron and is commanded by Lt Cdr Nigel May. She has just completed a deployment to the Baltic as part of the UK's MCM On Call Force where she worked with numerous NATO and PFP nations in several exercises. Built in Woolston, Southampton by Vosper Thorneycroft in 1998, she is the eighth of the Sandown Class of Single Role Minehunters to be accepted into the Royal Navy. This is the second ship to bear the name, the first HMS Grimsby was a sloop that was commissioned into service in 1934 and fought in the Second World War gaining Battle honours in Greece, Crete and Libya. On completion of the International Fleet Review Grimsby will be visiting her home town in Lincolnshire.

Shoreham

HMS Shoreham conducted NATO Squadron operations with MCMFORNORTH (Aug - Dec 04) as part of the UK's continuing commitment to NATO. Completing four months in the Baltic and visiting ports such as St Petersburg, Tallinn, Copenhagen - and many others. The NATO units conducted numerous exercises, including the multi-national mine hunting operation to clear former Word War Two mines from Baltic waters.

A successful period of Operational training from February to March followed, the ship achieving CincFleet's approval to conduct operations world-wide.

In April, after a short period of route-survey work in the Thames approaches the ship was the Second Sea Lords Flagship to commemorate the 100th Anniversary of the HMS Ganges Association. The weekend included the meeting with many fine maritime associations, including the Royal Navy Association, The British Legion and the Sea Cadets.

Participation in both the Mersey River Festival and the International Fleet Review have meant a very busy and high profile few weeks for Shoreham!

Patrol Craft

Tyne	**P281**

Displacement:	1,677 tonnes
Dimensions:	79.5 x 13.6 m
Propulsion:	2 x Ruston 12RK 270 Main
	Engines developing 4125kW
	@ 1000rpm; Controllable
	pitch propellers; 280kW Bow
	Thruster
Speed:	20 kts
Armament:	1 x 20mm BMarc gun;
	2 x General Purpose Machine
	Guns.
Complement:	30 (plus RM boarding team)

The three new River class Offshore Patrol Vessels are employed primarily in the Fishery Protection role with the capacity to operate in other areas. Fishery Protection duties include undertaking patrols in English, Welsh and Northern Ireland waters enforcing UK and EU fisheries legislation. Two man teams conduct boardings of fishing vessels inspecting net

HMS Tyne

sizes, weight of catches, fish sizes, composure of catches and the vessel's logbook and licence. The River class were built by Vosper Thornycroft (VT) in Southampton under an innovative arrangement, whereby the ships are leased to the Royal Navy under a five-year agreement which includes VT taking responsibility for maintenance and support during the period.

In operational terms, one of the major innovations is a large working cargo deck that allows the ships to be equipped with specific facilities for a particular role, such as disaster relief, anti-pollution, fire fighting, rescue work or interception of other vessels. A heavy crane with capacity for 25 tonnes is fitted to handle standard containers.

HMS Leeds Castle

Leeds Castle	P285	Explorer	P164
		Example	P165
Displacement:	1,450 tons	Archer	P264
Dimensions:	81 x 11 x 3 m	Tracker	P274
Propulsion:	2 ruston diesels driving two	Raider	P275
	shafts	Blazer	P279
Speed:	20 kts	Puncher	P291
Armament:	1 x 30mm gun.	Ranger	P293
Complement:	42	Trumpeter	P294

Commissioned in 1981 this Offshore Patrol Vessel has spent most of its life patrolling the waters around the Falklands Islands, a task she shared with her sistership Dumbarton Castle. She returned to the UK for the last time earlier this year and will shortly decommsiion, to be replaced by a new vessel, HMS Clyde, being built at Portsmouth by Vosper Thornycroft. Leeds Castle will be conducting patrol duties throughout the period of the Fleet Review.

Displacement:	54 tonnes
Dimensions:	20 x 5.8 m
Propulsion:	2 Perkins (RR) CV12 Turbo Diesels; 2 MTU V12 Diesels (Raider & Tracker)
Speed:	20-24 kts
Armament:	Can be fitted with GPMG.
Complement:	5 (Max 17)

The P2000 patrol craft are assigned to the 14

HMS Puncher

P201

MARITIME PHOTOGRAPHIC

University Royal Naval Units (URNUs), supporting the countries' leading Universities in England, Wales and Scotland . Their aim is to introduce a wide spectrum of high calibre undergraduates to the role of the Royal Navy, and to develop awareness of career opportunities in the Service. Each URNU is commanded by a RN Lieutenant who is responsible for 51 undergraduates who each join the URNU as RN Reservists for their 3 years at University. Training is conducted one evening a week in shore units at or near the University and at sea, over the weekends and during vacations, onboard a dedicated P2000 patrol craft.

The URNU/First Patrol Boat Squadron headquarters is a combined office at Portsmouth responsible for the administration and support of both the shore Units and the associated P2000 ships.

Two further ships of the class operate on security patrols in the waters around Cyprus.

Hydrographic Ships

Scott   H131

Displacement:	13,500 tons
Dimensions:	131.5 x 21.5 m
Propulsion:	2 x Krupp diesels, 1 shaft with controllable pitch propellors and a retractable bow thruster
Speed:	17.5 kts
Armament:	None
Complement:	63 (42 embarked)

Hydrographic and oceanographic surveying is the responsibility of the Royal Navy's Surveying Service, which has been operating throughout the world since the formation of the Hydrographic Department in 1795. The information from the surveys is used for producing Admiralty charts and nautical publications which have a world-wide sale and are used by ships of many nations.

HMS Scott

HMS Enterprise

NICK NEWNS

HMS Scott was constructed by Appledore Shipbuilders Ltd. in North Devon and launched on 13 October 1996.

The largest vessel in the flotilla she is fitted with a modern multi-beam sonar suite which permits mapping of the ocean floor worldwide. The ship is "lean-manned" with a complement of only 63, made possible by moving toward commercial manning practices like the use of fixed fire fighting equipment and extensive machinery and safety surveillance technology. The ship has a three watch crew rotation system with 42 personnel embarked at any one time, enabling the ship to operate abroad for extended periods. She was diverted earlier in the year to conduct seabed surveys off Indonesia in the wake of the Asian tsunami.

Armament: None
Complement: 46 (Max 81)

HMS Enterprise (and her sister HMS Echo) are two new multi-role Survey/Hydrographic/Oceanographic vessels which were built by Appledore Shipbuilders for the prime contractor Vosper Thorneycroft, both being launched in 2002.

Operationally available to the Commander in Chief Fleet for 330 days a year, survey work can be carried out for 90 per cent of the year due to improvements in seakeeping. They are able to collect an array of military hydrographic and oceanographic data and due to their multi-role capability are able to support mine warfare and amphibious operations.

Enterprise	H88
Displacement:	3,500 tons
Dimensions:	90.6 x 16.8 m
Propulsion:	Diesel electric propulsion; 3 main generators powering azimuth thrusters and a bow thruster.
Speed:	15 kts

Roebuck	H130
Displacement:	1,200 tonnes
Dimensions:	63.9 x 13 m
Propulsion:	4 Mirrlees Blackstone diesels; 2 shafts with controllable pitch propellors
Speed:	14 kts
Armament:	None

HMS Roebuck

NICK NEWNS

Complement: 46

HMS Roebuck is Commanded by Lieutenant Commander Jeremy Churcher and has a ship's company of 52 Officers and Ratings.

Built by Brooke Marine at Lowestoft, the ship entered service with the Royal Navy in July 1986. Built as a Coastal Survey Vessel primarily for surveying UK waters she has since seen extensive world-wide deployments from the Gulf to North America.

The ship has recently undergone an extensive refit and modernisation package in Devonport, which now sees her upgraded sufficiently to remain available to the Royal Navy for a further 10 years. The vessel's primary role consists of directed operational roles as a Fleet Unit in support of Amphibious Warfare (AW) operations, conducting Rapid Environmental Assessments (REA) (surveys to facilitate tactical exploitation of the environment by maritime and joint forces) and Mine Counter Measures Tasking

HMS Gleaner

MARITIME PHOTOGRAPHIC

MARITIME PHOTOGRAPHIC

Authority (MCMTA) support. These roles are in addition to her core output, Military Hydrographic Data gathering.

After completing operational training later this year, HMS Roebuck will be deploying to complete a series of hydrographic surveys and conduct further training with other RN ships.

Gleaner   H86

Displacement: 22 tonnes
Dimensions: 16 x 4.55 m
Propulsion: 2 x Volvo Penta diesels
Speed: 14 Kts
Armament: None
Complement: 8

HMSML Gleaner is the smallest commissioned vessel in the Royal Navy with a ship's company of only eight.

Commissioned on 5 December 1983 she is based at Devonport. She was designed to conduct inshore surveys along the south coast of England but has since spent time surveying around the entire coastline of Great Britain and visited various ports in Europe.

Gleaner is an advanced survey vessel, and uses multibeam and sidescan sonar to collect bathymetry and seabed texture data and compile an accurate and detailed seabed picture.

Endurance   A171

Displacement: 6,000 tonnes
Dimensions: 91 x 17.9 m
Propulsion: 2 Bergen diesels; 1 shaft with controllable pitch propellors and bow and stern thrusters
Speed: 14 kts
Aircraft: 2 x Lynx
Armament: None
Complement: 112 (plus 6 Royal Marines)

A Class 1 Icebreaker she was originally built in Norway in 1990 as MV Polar Circle. The RN chartered her in 1991 before she commissioned as HMS Polar Circle on 21 Nov 91. She was subsequently renamed HMS Endurance.

She deploys annually to the Antarctic, her operating area for 7 months of the year. Her base port is Portsmouth, which is also the ship's affiliated town.

She adds another string to her bow during the International Review as she takes on the role of

NICK NEWNS

a Royal Yacht, taking the Royal Party through the review lines.

Royal Fleet Auxiliaries

Wave Ruler   A390

Displacement:	30,300 tonnes (FL)
Dimensions:	196 x 27 x 10 m
Propulsion:	4 diesels; 1 shaft, bow and stern thrusters
Speed:	18 kts
Aircraft:	Can operate Merlin helicopters
Armament:	Fitted for 2 x Phalanx CIWS; 2 x 30 mm close range guns
Complement:	80 (plus 22 Fleet Air Arm personnel)

One of two large fleet tankers, RFA Wave Ruler is commanded by Captain Dale Worthington, who is regarded as the "owner" captain since the ship entered service in November 2003.

Wave Ruler returned to the UK in early March this year after 12 months on patrol in the West Indies as Atlantic Patrol (North) tanker supporting the on station frigate or destroyer. Last September Wave Ruler along with the frigate HMS Richmaond provided valuable technical and medical relief to Caribbean Islands in the aftermath of hurricanes IVAN and FRANCES. In January this year, she and her embarked Navy Lynx flight assisted by a permanent US Coast Guard detachment embarked, were involved in three seperate narcotic arrests seizing 4.8 tonnes of of cocaine - worth £200 million !

Since returning to the UK, the ship has been in Falmouth docks undergoing a major maintenance period and conducted continuation sea training off Plymouth prior to the International Fleet Review. After this review, the ship is representing the the Royal Fleet Auxiliary in its Centenary year by visiting Greenwich, Newcastle, Scarborough, Rosyth and Glasgow for a high profile "showing the flag" tour.

Wave Ruler will be retuning to the ATP (N) sta-

RFA Orangeleaf

tion in spring next year.

Orangeleaf A110

Displacement:	37,747 tonnes
Dimensions:	170 x 26 x 12 m
Propulsion:	2 Crossley-Pielstick diesels;
	1 shaft
Speed:	14.5 kts
Armament:	Fitted for 20 mm guns.
Complement:	60

RFA Orangeleaf is one of three ex-merchant ships, originally acquired for employment mainly freighting fuel between bases. All have been modified to enable them to refuel warships at sea. Orangeleaf is on long-term bareboat charter to the MoD but is to scheduled to decommission in 2008.

Fort Victoria A387
Fort George A388

Displacement:	31,500 tonnes
Dimensions:	204 x 30 x 9 m
Propulsion:	2 Crossley-Pielstick diesels;

RFA Fort Victoria

RFA Argus

	2 shafts
Speed:	20 kts
Aircraft:	Frequently deploy with up to
	three Merlin helicopters
Armament:	2 x Phalanx CIWS; 2 x 20mm
	close range guns.
Complement:	100 RFA; 24 MoD Civilians;
	32 RN and up to 122 Fleet
	Air Arm personnel.

"One stop" replenishment ships with the widest range of armaments, fuel and spares carried onboard. They can operate up to 5 Sea King or 3 Merlin helicopters (more in a ferry role) with full maintenance facilities onboard. Medical facilities have been upgraded with a 12 bed surgical capability to give the vessels a limited role as Primary Casualty Receiving Ships. Both are to remain in service until 2019.

RFA Fort Victoria is proud to be the RFA Flagship for the Review. She is commanded by Captain Bill Walworth, with a crew of RFA, Royal Navy and Civil Servants, from all over the country. The ship has spent the last few months working up and exercising after a major maintenance period last year. Most recently she took part in Exercise Loyal Mariner in the approaches to the Baltic, working with a large number of warships from NATO and partnership for peace nations. The ship provided logistic support to many of the units as well as simulating a variety of ships to exercise NATO units in maritime embargo operations. After a brief visit to Scotland, Fort Victoria spent a month with HMS Illustrious before making final preparations for the Review at Portland. She deploys to the Mediterranean in the Autumn.

After the Review she will move into Portsmouth Naval Base to take part in the International Festival of the Sea.

Argus   **A135**

Displacement:	28,081 tonnes
Dimensions:	175 x 30 x 8 m
Propulsion:	Electric drive; 2 Lindholmen-
	Pielstick diesel generator
	sets; 2 propulsion motors; 2
	shafts

Speed:	18 kts
Aircraft:	6 Sea King or Merlin; 12 Sea Harriers can be carried in the ferry role.
Armament:	4 x 30mm; 2 x 20mm close range guns
Complement:	254

Formerly the M/V Contender Bezant taken up from trade during the Falklands crisis. She was purchased in 1984 (£13 million) for conversion to an 'Aviation Training Ship'. A £50 million re-build was undertaken at Belfast from 1984-87. She undertook a rapid conversion in October 1990 to Primary Casualty Reception Ship for service in the Gulf. These facilities were upgraded and made permanent during 2001. Scheduled to decommission in 2008. A replacement for the Aviation Ship and PCRS role is currently under review. A new RFA PCRS is almost certain to be ordered, but probably not in a dual role as an Aviation ship and PCRS. If a new purpose-built/adapted ship is not acquired a likely scenario is that other RFAs with deck/hangar facilities are used for aviation training (as is the case now when ARGUS is unavailable) or the task may be carried out on RN ship flight decks.

Sir Bedivere   L3004

Displacement:	7,700 tonnes
Dimensions:	137 x 20 x 4 m
Propulsion:	2 diesels; 2 shafts; bow thrusters
Speed:	17 kts
Armament:	None
Complement:	65

Sir Galahad   L3005

Displacement:	8,451 tonnes
Dimensions:	140 x 20 x 4 m
Propulsion:	2 diesels; 2 shafts
Speed:	17 kts
Armament:	None
Complement:	58

Sir Tristram   L3505

Displacement:	5,550 tonnes
Dimensions:	126 x 18 x 4 m
Propulsion:	2 diesels; 2 shafts; bow thrusters

RFA Sir Bedivere

MARITIME PHOTOGRAPHIC

RFA Sir Galahad

Speed:	17 kts
Armament:	None
Complement:	65

Manned by the RFA but tasked by the Commodore Amphibious Task Group (COMATG), these ships are used for heavy secure transport of stores – embarked by bow

and stern doors. The can operate helicopters from both vehicle and flight deck if required and carry 340 troops. Sir Tristram was rebuilt after extensive Falklands War damage. After extensive delays, Sir Bedivere completed a Ship Life Extension Programme (SLEP) at Rosyth in 1998. These ships are occasionally used for MCMV support. Sir Galahad and Sir

MV Hurst Point

MARITIME PHOTOGRAPHIC

Tristram are to pay off in 2006 when they will be replaced by the new Bay class landing ships. Sir Bedivere is likely to continue in service.

Strategic Sealift Ro-Ro Ferry

MV Hurst Point

Displacement:	13,3000 tonnes (FL)
Dimensions:	193 x 26 x 6.6 m
Propulsion:	2 diesels; 2 shafts; bow thrusters
Speed:	18 kts
Armament:	None
Complement:	38

The contract for the supply of six ro-ro vessels to meet the requirements for stategic sealift capabilities was announced in October 2000. Under a 25 year private finance initiative deal, AWSR Shipping Limited were contracted to build and run the vessels for the MoD. The con-tract, likely to be worth up to £950 million, was finally signed on 27 June 2002. The MoD will normally use four of the ships, with all six available for operations. The unarmed ships have green hulls, white superstructure, yellow funnels and fly the Red Ensign.

Ramped Landing Craft

Aachen	**L110**
Arezzo	**L111**
Audemer	**L113**

Displacement:	165 tons
Dimensions:	33 x 8 x 1.5 m
Propulsion:	2 diesels; 2 shafts
Speed:	9 kts
Armament:	None
Complement:	6

These are Army owned landing craft operated by the Royal Logistic Corps.

SHIPS OF VISITING NAVIES
ATTENDING THE 2005 FLEET REVIEW

Country	Ship		Type
Algeria	EL KIRCH		Corvette
Australia	ANZAC	150	Frigate
Belgium	WESTDIEP	F911	Frigate
	NARCIS	M923	MCM
	GODETIA	A960	Support Ship
Brazil	CISNE BRANCO		Sail Training
Canada	MONTREAL	336	Frigate
Colombia	ARC GLORIA		Sail Training
Denmark	ESBERN SNARE	L17	Support Ship
Estonia	ADMIRAL PITKA	A320	Frigate
Finland	POHJANMAA	01	Minelayer
France	BELLE POULE		Sail Training
	MUTIN		Sail Training
	MEUSE	A607	Tanker
	CHARLE S DE GAULLE	R70	Aircraft Carrier
	JEAN BART	D615	Destroyer
	PERLE	S606	SSN
Germany	ASTA		Sail Training
	SACHSEN	F219	Frigate
	FRANKENTHAL	M1066	MCM
Greece	HYDRA	F452	Frigate
India	TARANGINI		Sail Training
	MUMBAI	D62	Destroyer
Indonesia	DEWA RUCI		Sail Training
Ireland	EITHNE	P31	Patrol Boat
Italy	AMERIGO VESPUCCI		Sail Training
	GIULIANO PRINI	S523	Submarine
Japan	KASHIMA	3508	Training Ship

	MURASAME	101	Destroyer
	YUUGIRI	153	Destroyer
Korea (South)	CHOONG MOO GONG YI SUN SHIN	975	Destroyer
	CHEONJI	57	Tanker
Latvia	VIRSAITIS	A53	Support Ship
Lithuania	KURSIS	M51	Minehunter
Morocco	MUHAMMED V	611	Frigate
Netherlands	URANIA		Sail Training
	ROTTERDAM	L800	Assault Ship
	URK	M861	Minehunter
Oman	SHABAB OMAN		Sail Training
	AL MUA'ZZAR	Q32	Frigate
Pakistan	TIPPU SULTAN	185	Frigate
	MOAWIN	20	Tanker
Poland	GENERAL T. KOZCIUSZKO	273	Frigate
	ISKRA		Sail Training
Portugal	ALVARES CABRAL	F331	Frigate
	SAGRES II		Sail Training
Romania	REGINA MARIA	F222	Frigate
Russia	ADMIRAL LEVCHENKO	605	Destroyer
Serbia	JADRAN		Sail Training
South Africa	DRAKENSBERG	A301	Support Ship
Spain	PRINCIPE DE ASTURIAS	R11	Aircraft Carrier
	BLAS DE LEZO	F103	Frigate
Turkey	ORU CREIS	F245	Frigate
Uruguay	CAPITAN MIRANDA		Sail Training
US Coast Guard	EAGLE		Sail Training
US Navy	CARL VINSON	CVN70	Aircraft Carrier
	ANTIETAM	CG54	Cruiser

HMAS Anzac

Algeria

El Kirch

Displacement:	560 tons
Dimensions:	59.3 x 12.6 x 2.4 m
Propulsion:	3 diesels driving 3 shafts
Speed:	30 kts
Armament:	2 x SS-N-2C Styx missiles or 16 x SS-N-25 Switchblade missiles; 1 x twin SA-N-4 Gecko missile launcher; 1 x twin 57 mm gun; 1 x 30mm gatling CIWS
Complement:	60

Rarely seen out of the Mediterranean several of the Soviet built Nanuchka class missile corvettes of the Algerian Navy have been recently modified with new generation surface to surface missiles.

Australia

Anzac   150

Displacement:	3,600 tonnes
Dimensions:	118 x 14.8 m
Propulsion:	1 x General Electric LM 2500 Gas Turbine; 2 x MTU diesels; 2 shafts with controllable pitch propellors.
Speed:	27 kts
Aircraft:	Seahawk helicopter
Armament:	1 x 5-inch Mk 45 Mod 2 automatic rapid fire gun; Sea Sparrow anti-air missile system; 2 x Mk 32 triple ASW torpedo tubes; 6 x 50 calibre machine guns.
Complement:	164

HMAS Anzac left her homeport of Fleet Base West on 7 March at the start of a six month deployment, visiting ports in Asia, Europe, the

BNS Narcis

United Kingdom and Africa. In addition to attending the Trafalgar 200 celebrations at Portsmouth highlights of her trip have included a passage from Albany to the Mediterranean, retracing the historic routes of the 1914 World War One convoys, culminating in services of Commemoration at Gallipoli.

NE Cisne Branco

Belgium

Westdiep   **F911**

Displacement:	1,880 tonnes
Dimensions:	103 x 12.3 m
Propulsion:	CODOG; 2 x V12 diesels and 2 x Rolls-Royce Olympus gas turbines; 2 shafts.
Speed:	26 kts
Armament:	4 x MM38 Exocet missiles; 1 x 100mm gun; 1 x Octuple Sea Sparrow missile launcher 1 x 375mm Bofors rocket launcher; 2 x 533mm torpedo tubes.
Complement:	156

Godetia   **A960**

Displacement:	1,700 tonnes
Dimensions:	91.83 x 14 x 3.5 m
Propulsion:	4 x High speed diesels; 2 shafts
Speed:	19 kts
Aircraft:	1 x Alouette III helicopter
Armament:	1 x 40mm Bofors; 6 x

	12.7mm Machine Guns.	Speed:	17 kts (under sail)
Complement:	95	Complement:	77

Narcis   M923

Displacement:	511 tonnes
Dimensions:	51.5 x 8.9 x 2.6 m
Propulsion:	1 x diesel; 1 controllable pitch propellor; 2 x bow thrusters; 2 x active rudders
Speed:	18 kts
Armament:	1 x 20mm close range gun
Complement:	45

Canada

Montreal   336

Displacement:	4,770 tonnes
Dimensions:	134.7 x 16.4 x 5
Propulsion:	2 x GE LM 2500 gas turbines; 1 x SEMT-Pielstick diesel; 2 shafts
Speed:	29 kts
Aircraft:	1 x Sea King
Armament:	2 x Quad Harpoon launcher; 2 x Sea Sparrow Octuple launcher; 1 x 57mm gun; 1 x Phalanx CIWS2 x twin torpedo tubes.
Complement:	198 (plus 17 aircrew)

Brazil

Cisne Branco   Sail Training Ship

Displacement:	1,038 tonnes
Dimensions:	60.5 x 10.5 x 4.8 m
Propulsion:	1 x diesel; 1 shaft

HMCS Montreal

ENS Admiral Pitka

DAVE CULLEN

Colombia

Gloria   Sail Training Ship

Displacement: 1,150 tonnes
Dimensions: 64.6 x 10.6 x 6.6 m
Propulsion: 1 x Auxiliary diesel
Speed: 10.5 kts
Complement: 51 (plus 88 trainees)

A Barque rigged sail training ship.

Denmark

Esbern Snare   L17

Displacement: 6,300 tonnes
Dimensions: 137.6 x 19.5 x 6.3 m
Propulsion: 2 x MTU 8000 Diesels; 2
                 shafts; 1 bow thruster
Speed: 23 kts
Aircraft: up to 2 Merlin helicopters
Armament: 1 x 5-inch Mk 45 Mod 4 gun;
                 4 x Harpoon SSM; Sea

Sparrow VLS Mk 48 Launcher (1x6) 7 x 12.7 mm Machine Gun
Complement: 100 (cabins for 169). Total
                 lodging capacity up to 300

Estonia

Admiral Pitka   A230

Displacement: 1,900 tonnes
Dimensions: 74.7 x 12.2 x 5.3 m
Propulsion: 3 diesels
Speed: 18 kts
Aircraft: Helicopter facilities
Armament: 1 x 3-inch gun
Complement: 43

The former Danish Naval vessel Beskytteren, a Modified Hvidbjørnen-class Command and Support Ship. She was built in 1975 at Aalborg Værft, Limjord, Denmark. Her hull is strengthened for ice operations.

ENS Admiral Pitka has been assigned to the

FNS Pohjanmaaa

Baltic Mine Countermeasures Squadron (BAL-TRON) as a staff and support ship on several occasions which has helped her crew gather valuable experience in co-operating with NATO forces.

From May 2005 to March 2006 ENS Admiral Pitka is assigned as the Command and Support Ship of Standing NATO Response Force Mine Countermeasures Group 1 (SNMCMG1) which is part of the NATO Response Force (NRF) maritime capability. She is the first vessel from the Baltic navies to be part of the force.

Finland

Pohjanmaa   01

Displacement:	1,400 tonnes
Dimensions:	78.5 x 11.7 x 3.5 m
Propulsion:	2 x Wärtsilä diesels; 2 shafts
Speed:	19 kts
Armament:	1 x 57mm; 2 x 40mm and 2 x small calibre twin barrelled guns
Complement:	135

FS Charles de Gaulle

The Finnish Navy minelayer Pohjanmaa was constructed by Wärtsilä shipyard, Helsinki in 1977 and commissioned on 8 June 1979, operating as a training ship for the Naval Academy until the end of 1992.

She underwent a major refit from 1997-1998 at Turku, Finland and was recommissioned on 12 February1998.

The Pohjanmaa has completed about 24 annual training trips, each trip lasting approximately two months. Before the Fleet review the ship had visited Cork in Ireland and Baltimore USA The current Commanding Officer is Lieutenant Commander Simo Laine.

France

Charles de Gaulle   R91

Displacement:	36,600 tonnes
Dimensions:	261.5 x 64.36 x 8.5 m
Propulsion:	Nuclear-Powered; 2 shafts
Speed:	27 kts
Aircraft:	35 - 40 (Super Etendard, Rafale, E-2 Hawkeye and helicopters)
Armament:	2 x Aster VLS missile systems; 2 x sextuple Sadral launchers; 8 x 20mm close range guns
Complement:	1,950

Jean Bart   D615

Displacement:	3,900 tonnes
Dimensions:	139 x 14 x 6.5 m
Propulsion:	4 x SEMT-Pielstick diesels: 2 shafts
Speed:	29.5 kts
Aircraft:	Lynx
Armament:	8 x MM40 Exocet missiles; 1 Standard missile launcher; 2 x sextuple Sadral systems; 1 x 100mm gun; 2 x 20mm close range;

Complement:	244

Meuse   A607

Displacement:	7,600 tonnes
Dimensions:	149 x 21.2 x 8.65 m
Propulsion:	2 x SEMT-Pielstick diesels; 2 shafts
Speed:	19 kts
Armament:	1 x 40mm; 2 x 20mm and 2 x 12.7mm machine guns.
Complement:	159

Perle   S606

Displacement:	2,400 tonnes
Dimensions:	73.6 x 7.6 x 6.4 m
Propulsion:	1 x CAS 48 pressurised water reactor; 1 shaft.
Speed:	25 kts
Armament:	4 x 533mm torpedo tubes capable of launching SM39 Exocet or torpedoes.
Complement:	132

Belle Poule   A650

Displacement:	227 tonnes
Dimensions:	32.45 x 7.4 x 3.65 m
Propulsion:	1 x Auxiliary diesel
Speed:	9 kts
Complement:	18 (plus 20 cadets)

A sail training ship.

Mutin   A652

Displacement:	57 tonnes
Dimensions:	33 x 6.4 x 3.4 m
Propulsion:	1 x Auxiliary diesel
Speed:	6 kts
Complement:	12 (plus 6 trainees)

A sail training ship.

FGS Sachsen

Germany

Asta

With an average utilization of 130 days, the 16 metre service Sloop Asta sails some 1,500 to 2,500 nm a year. After its major shipyard maintenance in 2004 it is one of the most modern sailing boats the German Navy has to offer. Electronic navigational chart, radar and bow thruster aid sailing the Asta. A new galley, a completely new electrical system with a 220 V shore power cable and a modern car radio were built in for a more convenient life on board. The boat is equipped with a GMDSS, shortwave receiver and satellite telephone to enable cruises outside the Baltic Sea

At the Naval Academy, Mürwik, the vessel is used for nautical extension training, long-distance cruises and full day cruises for both members of the Naval Academy and the German Navy.

Sachsen   F219

Displacement:	5,600 tonnes
Dimensions:	143 x 17.44 x 5 m
Propulsion:	CODAG; 1 x GE LM 2500 gas turbine; 2 x MTU diesels; 2 shafts
Speed:	29 kts
Aircraft:	2 x Lynx helicopters

HS Hydra

MARITIME PHOTOGRAPHIC

Armament:	1 x 76mm OTO Melara gun; 2 x Quad Harpoon missile launchers; 1 VL missile silo for ESSM and SM2 missiles; 2 x RAM launchers; 6 x torpedo tubes.
Complement:	255

Frankenthal   **M1066**

Displacement:	650 tonnes
Dimensions:	54.4 x 9.2 x 2.5 m
Propulsion:	2 diesels, 2 shafts
Speed:	18 kts
Armament:	1 x 40mm close range gun
Complement:	43

One of twelve Type 332 class coastal mine-hunters in service with the German Navy.

Spessart   **A1442**

Displacement:	14,200 tonnes
Dimensions:	130.15 x 19.4 x 8.2 m
Propulsion:	1 x diesel driving one shaft with a controllable pitch propellor.
Speed:	16 kts
Complement:	42

A small replenishment oiler purchased in 1976 and converted in 1977, entering German naval service in September of that year.

Greece

Hydra   **F452**

Displacement:	2,800 tonnes
Dimensions:	117.5 x 14.8 x 4.1 m
Propulsion:	CODOG; 2 x GE LM 2500 gas turbines; 2 x MTU diesels; 2 shafts
Speed:	31 kts
Aircraft:	Seahawk or AB212ASW
Armament:	2 x Quad Harpoon missile launchers; Sea Sparrow VLS system; 1 x 5-inch gun; 2 x Phalanx CIWS; 6 x torpedo tubes
Complement:	163

India

Mumbai   **D63**

Displacement:	6,700 tonnes
Dimensions:	163 x 17 x 6.5 m
Propulsion:	2 cruise diesels; 2 AM-50 boost gas turbines; 2 shafts
Speed:	28 kts
Aircraft:	2 Sea King
Armament:	2 SA-N-7 SAM (48 missiles total); 16 SS-N-25 SSM; 1 x 100 mm gun; 4 x 30 mm

ITS Guiliano Prini

DAVID HANNAFORD

close range guns, 2 x triple torpedo tubes

Complement: 360

Tarangini — Sail Training Ship

Displacement:	513 tonnes
Dimensions:	54 x 8.53 x 4.5 m
Propulsion:	2 Auxiliary Cummins Diesels
Speed:	11 kts
Complement:	36 (45 cadets)

A Three Masted Barque built by Goa Shipyard Limited Vasco Da- Gama, India in 1995, she was commissioned on 11 November 1997.
She has twenty sails (8 square and 12 fore and aft) covering a sail area of 965.4 sq. metres.

Indonesia

Kri Dewa Ruci — Sail Training Ship

Displacement:	1,500 tonnes
Dimensions:	136.2 x 31.2 x 13.9 m
Propulsion:	1 x MAN diesel
Speed:	10.5 kts
Complement:	110

Ireland

Eithne — P31

Displacement:	1,910 tonnes
Dimensions:	80.8 x 12 x 4.3 m
Propulsion:	2 x Ruston diesels; 2 shafts
Speed:	20+ kts
Aircraft:	1 x SA 365F Dauphin 2
Armament:	1 x 57mm Bofors gun; 2 x 20mm close range guns; 2 x GPMG
Complement:	73 (plus 8 aircrew)

Italy

Giuliano Prini — S523

Displacement:	1,662 tonnes (dived)
Dimensions:	64.4 x 6.8 x 5.6 m
Propulsion:	3 x Fincantieri diesels; 3 x generators; 1 x motor; 1 shaft
Speed:	11 kts (surfaced)
	19 kts (dived)
Armament:	6 x 21-inch torpedo tubes
Complement:	50

JDS Murasame

US NAVY

Amerigo Vespucci   **Sail Training Ship**

Displacement: 4,146 tonnes
Dimensions: 82.4 x 15.5 x 7 m
Propulsion: Diesel-electric; 1 shaft
Speed: 10 kts
Complement: 243

Japan

Kashima   3508

Displacement: 4,050 tonnes
Dimensions: 143 x 18 x 4.6 m
Propulsion: CODOG; 2 x Rolls-Royce
     Spey SM1C gas turbines; 2 x
     Mitsubishi diesels; 2 shafts
Speed: 25 kts
Aircraft: Platform for medium sized
     helicopter
Armament: 1 x 76mm OTO Melara gun;
     2 x 40mm saluting guns
Complement: 389

Murasame   101

Displacement: 5,100 tonnes (FL)

Dimensions: 151 x 17.4 x 5.2 m
Propulsion: COGAG; 2 x Rolls-Royce
     Spey SM1C gas turbines; 2 x
     GE LM 2500 gas turbines; 2
     shafts
Speed: 30 kts
Aircraft: 1 x SH-60J Seahawk
Armament: 2 x Quad Harpoon missile
     launchers; 16 cell Mk 48
     VLS missile system; 16 cell
     ASROC system; 1 x OTO
     Melara 76mm gun; 2 x
     Phalanx CIWS; 2 x triple
     torpedo tubes
Complement: 170

Yuugiri   153

Displacement: 4,200 tonnes (FL)
Dimensions: 137 x 14.6 x 4.5 m
Propulsion: COGAG; 4 x Rolls-Royce
     Spey SM1A gas turbines; 2
     shafts
Speed: 30+ kts
Aircraft: 1 x Sea King or Seahawk
Armament: 2 x Quad Harpoon missile
     launchers; Octuple Sea

LNS Virsaitis

Sparrow missile system;
Octuple ASROC system;
1 x OTO Melara 76mm gun;
2 x Phalanx CIWS; 2 x triple
torpedo tubes

Complement: 220

Latvia

Virsaitis A53

Displacement: 1,500 tonnes
Dimensions: 64.8 x 12 x 4 m
Propulsion: 2 x Wichmann Diesels.
Speed: 15 kts
Armament: 1 x 40mm close range gun
Complement: 55

Virsaitis is a Vidar class (Coastal minelayer), used as a staff and support ship. She was built in 1978, in Norway, and transferred to the Latvian Navy on 27 January 2003.
A member of BALTRON (Baltic MCM ships squadron) and has recently participated in exercise Royal Mariner (April 2005), and various Squadron exercises throughout March and May. The Fleet Review is part of a two month European tour which will end in July.

Lithuania

Kursis M51

Displacement: 470 tonnes
Dimensions: 47.1 x 8.3 m
Propulsion: 2 x diesels on 2 shafts with variable pitch propellers
Speed: 17 kts
Armament: 1 x 40mm Bofors gun
Complement: 42

The former German Lindau class minehunter Marburg, built in 1959 as a coastal minesweeper. By the mid 70s these vessels were converted to minehunters.

Morocco

Mohammed V 611

Displacement: 2,950 tonnes
Dimensions: 93.5 x 14 x 4.3 m
Propulsion: 4 diesels, 2 shafts
Speed: 20 kts
Aircraft: Panther helicopter
Armament: 2 x MM40 Exocet missiles, 1 x OTO Melara 76mm gun,

Mohammed V

US NAVY

HNLMS Rotterdam

MARITIME PHOTOGRAPHIC

| | 2 x 20 mm close range guns |
| Complement: | 80 |

Netherlands

Rotterdam   L800

Displacement:	12,000 tonnes
Dimensions:	160 x 25 x 5.9 m
Propulsion:	Diesel-electic; 4 diesels; 2 shafts
Speed:	20 kts
Aircraft:	Large flight deck and hangar
Armament:	2 x 30mm Goalkeeper CIWS, 4 x 20 mm close range gun
Complement:	113 (plus 600 troops)

Urk   M861

Displacement:	540 tonnes
Dimensions:	51.6 x 8.96 x 2.6 m
Propulsion:	1 diesel; 1 shaft
Speed:	15 kts
Armament:	1 x 20mm close range gun
Complement:	29-42

Urania   Sail Training Schooner

| Displacement: | 76 tonnes |

Dimensions:	23.9 x 5.3 x 3.2 m
Propulsion:	1 diesel
Speed:	5 kts diesel; 10 kts sail
Complement:	17

Oman

Al Mua'zzar   Q32

Displacement:	1,450 tonnes
Dimensions:	83.7 x 11.5 x 4.7 m
Propulsion:	4 diesels, 2 shafts
Speed:	25 kts
Aircraft:	Flight deck for small helicopter operations
Armament:	8 x MM40 Exocet SSM, 8-cell Crotale SAM, 1 x 76 mm OTO Melara, 2 x 20 mm close range guns
Complement:	80

Shabab Oman   Sail Training Ship

Displacement:	386 tonnes
Dimensions:	43.9 x 8.6 x 4.6 m
Propulsion:	2 x diesels; 2 shafts
Speed:	10 kts
Complement:	23 (plus 24 trainees)

PNS Tippu Sultan

Pakistan

Tippu Sultan   185

Displacement:	3,700 tonnes
Dimensions:	117.04 x 12.7 x 4.6 m
Propulsion:	2 Rolls-Royce Olympus gas turbines; 2 Rolls-Royce Tyne gas turbines; 2 shafts
Speed:	32 kts
Aircraft:	Alouette-III or Lynx helicopter
Armament:	4 x Harpoon SSM; 1 x 4.5-inch Mk 8 gun; 1 x Phalanx CIWS; 2 x triple ASW torpedo tubes
Complement:	180

The former Royal Navy Type 21 frigate HMS Active.

Moawin   A20

Displacement:	16,000 tonnes
Dimensions:	157 x 20.33 x 8.24 m
Propulsion:	Steam turbines; 2 boilers; 1 shaft
Speed:	20 kts
Aircraft:	Flight deck and hangar for up to 3 helicopters
Armament:	2 x 20mm close range guns
Complement:	200

Poland

General T. Kozciuszko   273

Displacement:	2,769 tonnes
Dimensions:	135.64 x 13.72 x 5.8 m
Propulsion:	2 x GE LM 2500 gas turbines; 1 shaft
Speed:	29 kts
Aircraft:	Sea Sprite helicopter
Armament:	1 x Mk13 Launcher (Harpoon and SM1 missiles);

ORP Iskra

	1 x 76mm OTO Melara gun; 1 x Phalanx CIWS; 2 x triple ASW torpedo tubes
Complement:	214

Iskra   Sail Training Ship

Displacement:	381 tonnes
Dimensions:	49 x 8 x 3.7 m
Propulsion:	1 x Auxiliary diesel
Speed:	10.2 kts
Complement:	13 (plus 50 cadets)

Portugal

Alvares Cabral   F331

Displacement:	3,200 tonnes
Dimensions:	115.9 x 14.8 x 5.97 m
Propulsion:	CODOG; 2 x MTU diesels; 2 x GE LM 2500 gas

NRP Alvares Cabral

RS Regina Maria

RFS Admiral Levchenko (with American cruiser in the background)

US NAVY

	turbines; 2 shafts
Speed:	31 kts
Aircraft:	Lynx
Armament:	2 x Quad Harpoon missile launchers; 1 x octuple Sea Sparrow missile launcher; 1 x 100mm gun; 1 x Phalanx CIWS; 2 x triple ASW torpedo tubes.
Complement:	192 (plus 16 flag staff)

Sagres II   Sail Training Ship

Displacement:	1,725 tonnes
Dimensions:	90 x 11.9 x 5.3 m
Propulsion:	2 MTU diesels; 1 shaft
Speed:	18 kts (under sail)
Complement:	162

Romania

Regina Maria   F222

Displacement:	4,850 tonnes
Dimensions:	148.1 x 14.75 x 4.3 m
Propulsion:	COGOG; 2 x Rolls-Royce Olympus gas turbines; 2 x Rolls-Royce Tyne gas turbines
Speed:	30 kts
Aircraft:	Large flightdeck and hangar
Armament:	1 x 76mm OTO Melara gun.
Complement:	246 (accomodation for 320)

Regina Maria is the former Royal Navy Type 22 frigate HMS London, which was paid off in 1998 as part of the Strategic Defence Review. The vessel has just been handed over and the crew are undegoing training prior to sailing for Romania in the Summer. A previous Regina Maria attended the 1937 Coronation Fleet Review at Spithead.

Russia

Admiral Levchenko   605

Displacement:	6,945 tonnes
Dimensions:	145 x 19 x 5.19 m
Propulsion:	COGAG; 2 x M-8KF gas turbines; 2 x M-62 gas turbines; 2 shafts
Speed:	29 kts
Aircraft:	2 Helix helicopters

Armament:	2 x quad SS-N-14 Silex ASW missiles; SA-N-9 Gauntlet missile system; 2 x 100mm guns; 4 x 30mm CIWS; 2 x 12 round RBU rocket launchers; 2 x quad torpedo tubes.
Complement:	220

Adventure

Adventure, a Nicholson 55 yacht, is a former Joint Services Adventurous Sail training Centre vessel which was gifted to the Russian Navy in July 2003 to mark the 300th anniversary of the Baltic Fleet and St Petersburg. The yacht was built for the Royal Navy in 1972 by Camper and Nicholson at Gosport

Serbia

Jadran   Sail Training Ship

Displacement:	737 tons

Dimensions:	48 x 8.9 x 4 m
Propulsion:	Burmeister-Alpha-Diesel
Speed:	10.4 kts
Complement:	61

A Barquentine built in 1933 and restored in 1946.

South Africa

Drakensburg   A301

Displacement:	12,500 tonnes (FL)
Dimensions:	147 x 19.5 x 7.9 m
Propulsion:	16, 320 hp(m) (12 MW); 1 shaft; cp prop; bow thruster
Speed:	20 + kts
Aircraft:	2 SA 330H/J Oryx
Armament:	4 x 20 mm close range guns; 6 x 12.7 mm Machine guns
Complement:	96 plus 10 aircrew plus 22 spare

SAS Drakensberg is the largest ship built in South Africa and the first naval vessel to be completely designed in country. In addition to

SAS Drakensberg

SPS Principe de Asturias

US NAVY

her replenishment role she is employed on search and rescue duties, patrol and surveillance duties and has considerable potential for use in disaster relief. As well as LCUs, she carries two diving support boats and two RHIBs. Replenishment at sea is from two abeam positions or from the RAS deck astern. She is also equipped for jackstay transfers and vertrep. She has two helicopter landing spots, one forward and one astern. Her main secondary role is the transport of consumables, but she can also be used to support small craft and transport a limited number of troops.

She sailed from Simon's Town on 6 June and made passage directly to the UK. En route home she will be visiting the African ports of Lagos (Nigeria) and Luanda (Angola) for diplomatic visits. She is expected to return to her homeport on 20 July.

South Korea

Chung Moo Gong Li Sun Shin   975

Displacement:	4,200 tonnes
Dimensions:	149.5 x 17.4 x 4.3 m
Propulsion:	CODOG; 2 x GE LM 2500 gas turbines; 2 x MTU diesels; 2 shafts
Speed:	30+ kts
Aircraft:	2 x Lynx
Armament:	2 x Quad Harpoon missile launchers; 4 x eight-cell Mk 41 VLS modules (SM-2MR and ASROC missiles); 1 x RAM system; 1 x 5-inch gun; 1 x Goalkeeper CIWS; 2 x triple torpedo tubes
Complement:	320

Cheon Ji 57

Displacement:	9,000 tonnes
Dimensions:	130 x 17.8 x 6.5 m
Propulsion:	2 diesels, 2 shafts
Speed:	20 kts
Aircraft:	Flight deck aft
Armament:	2 x twin 40 mm; 2 x 20mm
Complement:	Unknown

Spain

Principe de Asturias R11

Displacement:	16, 900 tonnes
Dimensions:	195.9 x 32 x 9.45 m
Propulsion:	2 LM2500 gas turbines; 1 shaft
Speed:	26 kts
Aircraft:	22 VSTOL and helicopters (10 Harrier, 6 Sea King ASW, 2 Sea King AEW, 4 AB-212)
Armament:	4 x 20 mm Meroka CIWS
Complement:	764

Blas de Lezo F103

Displacement:	4,555 tonnes
Dimensions:	146.72 x 18.6 x 4.75 m
Propulsion:	CODOG; 2 x GE LM 2500 gas turbines; 2 x diesels; 2 shafts
Speed:	28.5 kts
Armament:	2 x Quad Harpoon missile launcher; 48-cell Mk41 VLS (SM-2 and Evolved Sea Sparrow missiles); 1 x 5-inch gun; 1 x Meroka CIWS; 4 x fixed torpedo tubes.
Aircraft:	SH-60B Seahawk
Complement:	250

Turkey

Oru Creis F245

Displacement:	3,100 tonnes
Dimensions:	116.72 x 14.8 x 6.12 m
Propulsion:	CODOG; 2 x MTU diesels; 2 x GE LM 2500 gas

TCG Oru Creis

NICK NEWNS

USCG Eagle

US COASTGUARD

turbines; 2 shafts
Speed: 31.75 kts
Aircraft: AB-212ASW Helicopter
Armament: 2 x Quad Harpoon missile launcher; 1 x Octuple Sea Sparrow missile launcher; 1 x 5-inch gun; 3 x Sea Zenith CIWS; 2 x triple ASW torpedo tubes.
Complement: 180

Uruguay

Capitan Miranda **Sail Training Ship**

Displacement: 587 tonnes
Dimensions: 54,6 x 8.4 x 3.6 m
Propulsion: 1 x auxiliay diesel
Complement: 49

United States Coast Guard

USCG Eagle **Sail Training Ship**

Displacement: 1,519 tonnes
Dimensions: 89.92 x 11.92 x 5.18 m
Propulsion: 1 x Caterpillar diesel
Speed: 17 kts (under sail)
Complement: 65 (plus 175 cadets and instructors)

United States Navy

(As we went to press the presence of the US Navy vessels was still unconfirmed).

Carl Vinson **CVN70**

Displacement: 78,172 tons (101,089 FL)
Dimensions: 334.7 x 40.85 x 12.5 m
Propulsion: 2 x GE A4W pressurised

USS Carl Vinson

USS Antietam

water nuclear reactors;
4 x geared steam turbines
driving 4 shafts

Speed: 31.5 kts
Aircraft: 48 x F-14/FA-18; 4 x EA-6B;
                 4 x E-2C; 7 x SH-60F
Armament: 3 x Octuple Sea Sparrow
                 missile launchers; 4 x
                 Phalanx CIWS
Complement: 5,802 (including Air Wing)

The ten nuclear-powered aircraft carriers of the Nimitz class, of which Carl Vinson was the third one built in 1982, are the largest warships ever built.

Antietam   **CG54**

Displacement: 7,242 tons
Dimensions: 172.46 x 16.76 x 7.46 m
Propulsion: 4 x GE LM2500 gas turbines;
                 2 shafts
Speed: 30+ kts
Aircraft: Up to 2 SH-60B
Armament: 2 x Mk 41 VLS (Tomahawk,
                 Standard and ASROC
                 missiles); Up to 8 Harpoon
                 missiles; 2 x 5-inch guns; 2 x
                 Phalanx CIWS; 2 x 25mm
                 close range guns; 4 x 12.7mm
                 machine guns; 2 x Triple
                 ASW tubes.
Complement: 387

FLYPAST OF MILITARY AIRCRAFT

Up to 86 aircraft from around the world will flypast the fleet at 5.30 pm on 28 June.

They will be lead by the Royal Navy Sea Harriers - fast disappearing from service as a result of recent defence cuts.

NICK NEWNS

TALL SHIPS AND MERCHANT SHIPS ATTENDING THE REVIEW

Bulgaria	KALIAKRA	Tall Ship
France	LA RECOUVRANCE	Topsail Schooner
	RENARD	Topsail Cutter
	RARA AVIS	Tall Ship
Denmark	GEORG STAGE	Tall Ship
Ireland	TS ASGARD II	Tall Ship
Netherlands	TS ARTEMIS	Tall Ship
	TS EUROPA	Tall Ship
	TS MERCEDES	Tall Ship
	SWAN MAKKUM	Tall Ship
	IRIS	Tall Ship
Norway	TS SORLANDET	Tall Ship
Poland	DAR MLODZIEZY	Tall Ship
	POGORIA	Tall Ship
Russia	MIR	Tall Ship
USA	PRIDE OF BALTINMORE	Tall Ship
UK	GRAND TURK	Tall Ship
	ROYALIST	Tall Ship
	LORD NELSON	Tall Ship
	TENACIOUS	Tall Ship
	PRINCE WILLIAM	Tall Ship
	MATTHEW	Tall Ship
	EARL OF PEMBROKE	Tall Ship
	KASKELOT	Tall Ship
	PHOENIX	Tall Ship
	BESSIE ELLEN	Tall Ship
	WILL	Sailing Barge
	SLOOP PICKLE	Tall Ship
	SHIELDHALL	Preserved Steamer
	JOHN JERWOOD	Sea Cadets Corps
	BALMORAL	Preserved Steamer
	KITTY	Sailing Barge
	PRINCESS CAROLINE	Hospitality Vessel

Sea Cadets	JOHN JERWOOD	
Red Funnel Lines	RED JET 4	
	RED EAGLE	
Dredger	SAND HARRIER	
Survey Vessel	SEA VIGIL	
Charity Vessel	AMAZON HOPE	
Charity Vessel	PRIDE OF BRISTOL	
RNLI	SEVERN CLASS	Lifeboat
	TRENT CLASS	Lifeboat
	ATLANTIC 75	Lifeboat
B.A.S.	RV JAMES CLARKE ROSS	
Sir Donald Gosling	MY LEANDER	
Northern Lighthouse Board	PHAROS	
Cunard	QUEEN ELIZABETH 2	
Silver Sea Cruises	SILVER CLOUD	
BP Shipping	BRITISH MERLIN	
Global Marine	SOVEREIGN	
HM Customs	VIGILANT	
SFPA	NORNA	
Guernsey Sea Fisheries	LEOPARDESS	
Historic Vessels	MTB 102	
	HMS MEDUSA	
	RAF SPT 206	
	TUG CHALLENGE	
	TUG BROCKLEBANK	
	FV JACINTA	

Kaliakra

Bulgaria

Kaliakra

Kaliakra trains future officers for the Bulgarian Navy and is the sistership to Iskra. She is based at Varna on the Black Sea, but often travels to Europe and America for the Cutty Sark Tall Ships' Races.

France

La Recouvrance

La Recouvrance was built in Brest, France, in 1992 and is a replica of a French military ship of the 19th century. She was built as part of national competition amongst coastal ports to build a ship traditional to their area. The city of Brest set about building the Recouvrance to the

plans of vessels, known as type 'IRIS', used as military dispatch vessels.Originally carrying some 50 to 60 men, the Recouvrance now carries 12 passengers for overnight voyages and 25 for day sails.

Renard

Le Renard was built in St Malo in 1991 as part of the French maritime regeneration project 'Les Bateaux des Cotes de France'. Every French port was asked to build a replica of their traditional vessel. St Malo chose a Corsair Cutter reflecting its days as a pirate fortress.

Rara Avis

The Rara Avis was built in 1957, inspired by the design of a Thames barge. In 1995 the ship was completely refitted at her home-port of Brest with finances raised by the local community and the work carried out by some 70 trainees. Today this attractive schooner offers comfortable cabins, a lower saloon and a lovely deckhouse saloon for entertaining. Rara Avis regularly sails around the French coast and makes annual trips across the Atlantic with her sistership, Bel Espoir.

Denmark

Georg Stage

The full-rigged training ship built in 1934 Georg Stage is owned and run by The Georg Stage Memorial Foundation (Georg Stages Minde) - established in 1882 by Mr. Carl Frederik Stage, a Danish shipowner, and his wife Thea. They donated a fully equipped training ship, and later bequeathed a sum of money to support the running of the ship, which was named after their only son, Georg Stage, who died at the age of 22 years.

The aim of the foundation is ". . . to give young people wishing to go to sea, their first lesson in practical seamanship aboard a purpose-built training ship", in other words an entry-level course in seamanship for professional seamen. To replace the first training ship the present Georg Stage was built in 1934/35 and entered service in April 1935. Today the ship carries 63 cadets.

Ireland

TS Asgard II

Asgard II, a brigantine, was designed by Jack Tyrell specifically for sail training and built at Arlow, County Wicklow in 1981. Asgard II's figurehead is a carving of Granuaille, the famous 16th century Mayo sea captain and pirate queen of the sea.

TS Asgard II

MARITIME PHOTOGRAPHIC

TS Artemis

The original Asgard, a gaff rigged ketch, was designed and built in Norway by Colin Archer of Larvick in 1905 as a wedding present to Mary Hamilton Osgood, from her parents, on her marriage to Erskine Childers, father of the late President Childers. The name Asgard is an old Norse word meaning 'Home of the Gods'.

In July 1914, Asgard with Erskine, his wife Mary, and four others sailed to the North Sea to collect a cargo of guns, which had been bought in Hamburg for the Irish Volunteers. After a difficult voyage the cargo was landed in Howth on 26 July 1914.

Asgard was sold in 1926 and passed through several hands before being purchased by the Irish Government in 1961 because of her historical associations. In 1968 the Government formed the committee known as Coiste An Asgard and placed Asgard under their guidance and control to be used as a sail training vessel for the young people of Ireland. Sail training cruises were carried out on Asgard each year from 1969 to 1974 until she was transferred to Kilmainham Jail Historical Museum in 1979 for exhibition to the public.

Netherlands

TS Artemis

The Frisian Sailing Company's new flagship was given the name Artemis when she was launched in 1926. Equipped as a whaling vessel, she hunted whales until the end of the 1940's. She chiefly navigated the Artcic and Antarctic Oceans.

In the 1950's, she was converted into a freighter and sailed mainly between Asia and South America. During these voyages, however, her home port remained Marstal, Denmark.

Further Information at:
www.tallship-artemis.com

TS Europa

The Europa was built in 1911 and started life as a light ship. In 1994 she was fully re-built as a barque and now roams the oceans of the world in the best seafaring tradition. This beautiful ship has a traditional mahogany deckhouse, teakwood decks as well as the beautiful interior with authentic early 20th century details providing the perfect ambiance for a fantastic voyage. All cabins are provided with en-suite shower and toilet and there is also a hospital, deck lounge with bar, mess room and a library. The Europa's voyages regularly take her as far afield as the Antarctic, Argentina and South Africa then back again to Europe and the UK. These amazing voyages are available to individual customers looking for a fantastic ocean adventure. From time to time the Europa is also available for corporate charters and day sails.

Further Information at:
www.barkeuropa.com

TS Mercedes

The Mercedes is the newest tall ship to be built being launched in the Netherlands in April 2005. Above deck the ship has a traditional brig rig with a total of 18 sails and spacious open decks. Below deck Mercedes is far from traditional. From the first deck you enter the bar - a light and spacious area with fantastic views out over the sea. From here there is an elegant staircase down to the main saloon/restaurant. The Mercedes can carry up to 130 guests for a day sail and 150 guests at the quayside. With seating for up to 60 guests the ship is suitable for dinners, conferences and lectures and is fitted with the latest multimedia technology.

Iris

Iris was built in 1916 and is a fine example of the last generation of sailing luggers. In 1929 she received her first engine and was converted into a commercial trading vessel, then based in Denmark. She sailed for 40 years on the Baltic Sea.
Restored to her former glory in 1981 she now sails under the Dutch flag for the second time in her life. From her homeport of Rotterdam Iris

cruises all over NW Europe offering sailing holidays, day sails, corporate events and is a regular at the major maritime festivals.
The traditional appearance and historical importance of the ship are perfectly balanced with the modern demands of comfort and safety. Iris is a fast, comfortable ship providing great entertainment on the water.

Swan Fan Makkum

The world's largest brigantine, Swan fan Makkum is a unique vessel. She was built as an exact 19th-century replica in 1993, a true windjammer with her fourteen sails totalling over 1300 square metres.
During the summer she undertakes cruises, film work and management training in European waters, from the Channel to the Baltic. In winter months, she sets sail for the Caribbean, an appropriate setting for such an extraordinarily beautiful ship.

Norway

TS Sorlandet

Sørlandet was formerly a schoolship for training young cadets, but is now owned and operated by a non profit foundation, controlled and partly funded by the Norwegian Department of Culture. She is the oldest of the three Norwegian Tall Ships; built in Kristiansand and launched in 1927. On her maiden voyage to Oslo in 1927, Sørlandet was inspected by HM King Haakon and Crown Prince Olav. One of her highlights was the cruise to the World Fair in Chicago in 1933.
Being the first Norwegian training ship to cross the Atlantic, she actually served as the Norwegian pavilion during the exhibition "A Century in Progress".
Sørlandet was damaged during World War II where she, among other things, served as an accommodation vessel for German sub-

mariners. She was restored and was ready to sail in 1948, but it wasn't until 1958 that she was equipped with an engine and propeller.

In 1974 she was sold and laid up for three years until 1977 when she was bought back to Kristiansand. From 1981 she has been owned by the non-profit foundation Stiftelsen Fullriggeren Sørlandet.

From 1980 to 1983, Sørlandet was the only Norwegian training ship still operating and at that time the open cruises for both sexes, all ages and nationalities started. She crossed the Atlantic four times in 1981, was used for a film shoot in New York and performed several cruises between Bermuda and Boston.

In 1986, she once again crossed the Atlantic to take part in the 100th Anniversary of the Statue of Liberty in New York.

Towards Sørlandet's 70th Anniversary in 1997, she worked closely in co-operation with the Royal Norwegian Navy, Norwegian Shipowners Association and the local public Employment Office, doing six-week courses in sailing and general seamanship in order to boost the recruitment of seafarers.

Further Information at:
www.fullriggeren-sorlandet.no

Poland

Dar Mlodziezy

Dar Mlodziezy has been owned by the Gdynia Maritime Academy since she was built in 1982, replacing the frigate Dar Pormoza which had trained future officers of the merchant and fishing fleets for over fifty years.

Dar Mlodziezy has taken part in the Cutty Sark Tall Ships' Races many times; Her debut was in 1982 when she crossed the start line directly after being commissioned. Shortly after, she began a circumnavigation of the globe which coincided with the 200th anniversary of

Australia.

Pogoria

The fully rigged ship Pogoria was built in 1980 for the Iron Shackle Fraternity - a marine educational project which was conceived and founded by Captain Adam Jasser in 1971. The project was later sponsored by Polish National Television, and the TV Magazine 'Flying Dutchman'.

The current owner and operator of Pogoria is the Sail Training Association of Poland. She is 154 feet long overall with accommodation for up to 50 crew and students.

Russia

Mir

Mir, which means Peace, was built as the third of five sister ships at the Lenin-shipyard in Gdansk, Poland, based on a new type of design for square rigged training vessels. The first ship of this design was called Dar Mlodziezy, which was built to replace the old sail training ship Dar Pormoza for the Polish merchant navy. Russia then decided that she wanted a similar design for five ships as part of a trading deal with Poland. First came Druzhba and then in 1987 Mir for which the rigging design was slightly altered so that she could sail closer to the wind - up to 30 degrees rather than the usual 60 degrees for square riggers.

Mir's full complement of sails is 26. She has sailed with a crew of 200 but can be sailed with as few as 30.

USA

Pride of Baltimore II

A topsail schooner built along the lines of the 1812 era Baltimore Clippers. She promotes tourism and economic development for

TS Pogoria

MARITIME PHOTOGRAPHIC

Maryland and Baltimore, internationally. She also aids Maryland's students through a special electronic curricula using the internet.

Further Information at:
www.marylandspride.org

UK

Grand Turk

The Grand Turk is a replica 18th Century man-of-war of the type that took part in the Battle of Trafalgar. Built in 1996, her primary role is in the film and television industry where she has featured in such programmes as Hornblower and Longitude.

In addition to film work, the Grand Turk makes a stunning venue for entertaining. Her spacious saloon is a great place for entertaining and can seat up to 120 people for dinner. On deck her traditional rigging and numerous cannons provide the backdrop for receptions for up to 200 people at the quayside.

Grand Turk

Royalist

Built in 1971 by Groves and Gutteridge in Cowes, Isle of Wight to a design by Colin Mudie. The Sea Cadets new brig was named Training Ship Royalist by HRH Princess Anne on 3 August 1971.

In 1992, Princess Anne attended the rededication of Royalist after an extensive refit in Lymington.Royalist is owned and operated by the Sea Cadet Association and the ship provides about 800 cadets with berths each year.

Further Information at:
www.sea-cadets.org

Lord Nelson

Named after the British Admiral, Lord Nelson was launched in 1985 and is one of two specifically designed vessels run by the Jubilee Sailing Trust in Southampton for able-bodied and physically disabled people to share the adventure and experience of tall ship sailing. The Trust commissioned Colin Mudie to design the first sailing ship in which physically disabled people comprised half the crew. Requirements included wheelchair access throughout the ship, light hauling loads on the ropes and better than usual protection against the cold and wet.

The three masted square-rigged, Lord Nelson

Lord Nelson

was the result. Her steel hull is coated with special paint for long-life, her spars are stable and she was extensively refitted with roller-furling sails, reducing the number of crew needed to go aloft. Overall, Lord Nelson has been designed to adapt to the needs of most disabilities and to sail in any sea around the world.

She took part in all legs of Tall Ships 2000, racing for the first time ever in the trans-Atlantic Race from Cadiz to Bermuda.

Further Information at:
www.jst.org.uk

Tenacious

Tenacious is the largest wooden tall ship of her kind in the world. The innovative wood epoxy laminate build started in 1996 with a team made up of skilled designers, engineers, shipwrights and fitters. These were supplemented by a volunteer force of over 1500 able bodied and disabled people who came on working shorewatch holidays from all over the UK and abroad.

Since commencing voyages in September 2000, Tenacious has taken 3,652 people to sea. Of these 1,428 were physically disabled and 5167 were wheelchair users.

The ship has access throughout for disabled crew, including wheelchair users, with flat wide decks and powered lifts. There is a speaking compass for the use of blind crew members and bright track radar for partially sighted crew. An induction loop and vibrator alarms have been installed for hard of hearing crew members.

Prince William

Commissioned by the Tall Ships Youth Trust in 2001 and is the newest tall ship to be built in the UK. Built by Appledore Ship Yard, she is very proud to be the first vessel to be named after His Royal Highness.

Together with her sister ship Stavros S Niarchos, these brigs were specifically built as sail training vessels for young people aged 16-25. The two brigs take over 2,500 young people to sea every year and as one of the oldest sail training organisations, the Tall Ships Youth Trust's experience in personal development through tall ship sailing can guarantee to bring the best out of her crew during the tall ships races!

During the finale of 2002 Cutty Sark Tall Ship Race Stavros S Niarchos led the fleet out into the Solent for the Parade of Sail with a crew of 48 young people from the Portsmouth area.

Matthew

Over 500 years ago John Cabot and his crew set sail for Asia aboard the original Matthew hoping to trade goods and commodities with the people who lived there.

However, he finally arrived on the coast of Newfoundland and therefore was the original discoverer of America, not Christopher Columbus as most people are led to believe.

Today the replica of the Matthew sits proudly in Bristol harbour for all to see. The general public are able to board The Matthew as well as embark on trips around the harbour.

In 1997 the replica Matthew followed the same course as John Cabot in 1497 and sailed across to Newfoundland. She carried the same number of crew members as the original and took the same amount of time to complete the crossing.

Earl of Pembroke

Earl of Pembroke was originally named Orion and was built in Pukavik, Sweden in 1948.

She traded timber in the Baltic and British East Coast until being laid up in Denmark in 1974.

The company Square Sail of Charlestown, Cornwall, purchased her in 1979 and in 1985 she underwent a complete restoration programme.

In 1994 she was commissioned as the three masted 18th century wooden Barque that she is today.

Prince William

MARITIME PHOTOGRAPHIC

Matthew

Kaskelot

A replica 19th century 3 masted Barque, one of the largest remaining wooden ships in commission. Built in 1948 for the Royal Greenland Trading Company supplying the remote East Greenland coastal settlements. Subsequently she was employed as a fisheries support vessel in The Faroes.

Square Sail purchased the vessel in 1981 and totally redesigned and re-rigged her.

Phoenix

Built by Hjorne & Jakobsen at Frederikshavn, Denmark in 1929 as an Evangelical Mission Schooner, 20 years later she retired from missionary work and carried cargo until her engine room was damaged by fire. She was bought by new owners in 1974 who converted her into a Brigantine before being purchased by Square Sail in 1988. A first aid over-haul enabled her to sail back to the UK where she underwent a complete refit.

Bessie Allen

Launched in 1907, Bessie Ellen is one of the last remaining examples of the schooners and ketches of the West Country, which in the latter part of last century, and up until the 1930's carried cargo around the coasts of the United

Kingdom and Europe.

Will

Built as Will Everard in 1925 by Fellowes at Great Yarmouth, for F.T. Everard's, this steel barge was built to a plan and was one of 4 almost identical barges, the others being Alf Everard, Ethel Everard and Fred Everard.

By 1995 she was the only one of the four sister ships left and was owned by P & O Shipping Line. Re-named Will, she was used as corporate publicity vessel under Capt. Susan Harrison, who subsequently bought the vessel in early summer 1998.

The vessel is now normally moored in historic St. Katharine Docks, London.

Sloop Pickle

In celebration of the 200th anniversary of the Battle of Trafalgar and of Admiral Lord Nelson's death, there are many events being organised for the summer of 2005. One of these is the New Trafalgar Dispatch.

The New Trafalgar Dispatch is a recreation of the delivery of Vice Admiral Collingwood's original dispatch (report) to the Admiralty following the battle. The original dispatch was carried by HM Schooner Pickle from the fleet off Cape Trafalgar to Falmouth From there the Lieutenant commanding HMS Pickle travelled by post chaise to London with the news.

The recreation comprises a voyage in the summer of 2005 by the Jubilee Sailing Trust's ship, the Lord Nelson, from Cape Trafalgar to

Kaskelot

Sloop Pickle

SS Shieldhall

Falmouth following HMS Pickle's track. A specially built replica post chaise will then travel on parts of the route of the original 1805 journey from Falmouth to London, now known as the Trafalgar Way, arriving at the Admiralty in London in September 2005. Events have been organised in the towns and villages along the Trafalgar Way.

Kitty

One of 37 barges built in Gas House Creek, Harwich, Kitty was built in 1895 by J & H Cann. A Shipwright renowned for both high quality workmanship and a reputation for building fast vessels. Kitty carries the evidence with a collection of 1st, 2nd and 3rd place plaques from the Thames, Medway and East Coast barge matches during the 1970's.

25 metres in length, with a 6.5 metre beam; Kitty is massively built on oak frames and floors and clad in 3 and 4 inch pitch pine. She still has her original pine keelson 0.4 metres square and 23 metres long. Her spritsail rig has a sail area of almost 3000 square feet and her gross tonnage is 79 tons; she is capable of car-

rying a cargo of 150 tons.

Kitty is now owned by S.B.Kitty Ltd and engages in the passenger charter trade where she is used for both private and corporate events. Whether sailing within the Solent, crossing the channel or simply enjoying her facilities moored alongside the Boardwalk at Port Solent, Portsmouth, Kitty offers her visitors a unique experience.

Shieldhall

SS Shieldhall is the largest remaining steam powered general cargo-passenger ship in the world. She was laid down in October 1954 and entered service in October 1955. Built by Lobnitz & Co., of Renfrew, she is of riveted and welded construction with a straight stem and a cruiser stern.

She was operated by Glasgow Corporation to transport treated sewage sludge down the river Clyde to be dumped at sea. She continued a tradition, dating back to the First World War, that Glasgow's sludge vessels carried organised parties of passengers when operating during the summer months. Thus Shieldhall was built with accommodation for 80 passengers.

In 1976, after 21 years of faithful service she was laid up before being purchased by the Southern Water Authority in 1977. After minor modifications, she carried sludge from Southampton to an area south of the Isle of Wight for five years from 1980.

As a result of an initiative by the Southampton City's Museum Services, a preservation society was formed and Shieldhall was purchased from Southern Water in 1988, for £20,000.

Much work is done on the ship by a dedicated group of volunteers in order to keep her in sea-going condition. The saloon has been restored and the galley brought up-to-date. Crewed by volunteers, she is a frequent sight around the Solent running excursions and such like. She has been to Holland for the Dordrecht Steam Festival and she has been an attendee at each of the earlier International Festivals of the Sea at Bristol and Portsmouth.

During the summer months, various excursions are run in the Solent area and during the course of these voyages, passengers are encouraged to visit the Bridge and machinery spaces.

John Jerwood

TS John Jerwood, is a 24-metre power-training ship operated by the Sea Cadet Corps, which came into service in 2002.

The Jerwood Foundation's award of £1,216,700 to the Sea Cadets towards the funding of a new off-shore power training vessel was announced in March 2000. The Sea Cadets run a training programme for 10-18 year olds, teaching team-work and social responsibility through a range of activities based on seamanship and maritime skills. The two former training vessels, which served the 400 cadet units nation-wide, were decommissioned in 1998 as they failed to meet new safety regulations. TS John Jerwood enables the cadets to offer power boat experi-ence to trainees, a crucial part of their instruc-tion.

The TS John Jerwood was officially named at a

John Jerwood

Princess Caroline

ceremony in September 2002 by The Second Sea Lord and Commander in Chief Naval Home Command Vice Admiral Sir Peter Spencer KCB ADC
She has berths for 12 Cadets and two adults, with a permanent crew of four.

Princess Caroline

Built in 1980, the Princess Caroline started life as a passenger vessel ferrying pasengers around the various ports along the Portuguese coast. Completely refurbished in 2003, this motor cruiser is now available for charter and corporate hire in the UK.
The 193 ton vessel is attending the review as the host ship of the charity Seafarers UK (the former King George's Fund for Sailors)

Balmoral

Balmoral was built in Southampton in 1949 and operated under the Southampton Red Funnel Fleet for 20 years. She then moved round to the Bristol Channel where she became the last member of P&A Campbell's famous White Funnel Fleet. When they ceased operation in 1980, the ship moved to Dundee to become a floating restaurant but gradually fell into disrepair, until she was rescued by the friends & supporters of the paddle steamer Waverley.
She returned to service in 1986 and now operates her main summer season in the Bristol Channel, offering day excursions to popular Coastal Resorts, as well as making visits to other ports & piers throughout the UK in Spring & Autumn. For more detailed information on the Balmoral, please visit the website at www.pswaverley.org.

RNLI

The blue and orange hulled lifeboats of the RNLI are perhaps the most recognisable of vessels seen around the UK coastline.
Sir William Hillary, a courageous lifeboatman,

Balmoral

co-ordinated the first lifeboat service in 1824. His appeal to the nation led to the foundation of the National Institution for the Preservation of Life from Shipwreck, later to become the Royal National Lifeboat Institution.

The RNLI today is a registered charity committed to saving lives at sea. It provides, on call, the 24-hour lifeboat search and rescue service to 50 miles out from the coast of the United Kingdom and the Republic of Ireland, and a beach lifeguard service on 57 beaches in the south west of England. The RNLI continues to rely on voluntary contributions and legacies for its income.

There are 232 lifeboat stations strategically placed around the UK and Republic of Ireland. The RNLI is represented at the review by a Severn class lifeboat. These vessels were first introduced in 1996 and the vessel at the review is the last of the class to be built. At 17 metres

Severn Class Lifeboat

the Severn class are the largest of the fleet and designed to standby afloat. They carry their own inflatable which can be launched and recovered by a lightweight framework and winch.

Also present at the review is a 14 metre Trent class vessel. Again designed to standby afloat at deep water moorings or at a berth.

Of interest the hull numbers on RNLI lifeboats give class and vessel information. The first two figures are the length of the boat in metres, so the 17 m Severn class all begin with 17, and the second two numbers denote which member of the class. Therefore 17-20 is the 20th Severn class and 14-09 is the ninth of the 14 metre Trent class.

Red Jet 4

One of the most common sights along the Solent are the red hulled ferries and passenger vessels of the Red Funnel Line. Red Jet 4 is a 39m catamaran ferry which was built in Tasmania in 2003. Powered by 2 externally silenced turbocharged diesels driving two vector controlled water jets these vessels can deliver 275 passengers from Southampton to West

Trent Class Lifeboat

RNLI

Cowes on the Isle of Wight in 22 minutes at speeds up to 35 knots.

Red Jet 4

RED FUNNEL LINES

Red Eagle

Red Eagle

Red Eagle is one of Red Funnel Line's car and passenger ferries plying the route between Southampton and East Cowes. Built by Ferguson Shipbuilders, this 4,075 tonne vessel can carry 200 cars and up to 895 passengers. Powered by two turbo diesels capable of driving the vessel at 14 knots the crossing time is around 55 minutes.

BP British Merlin

Built in 2003 by Samsung Heavy Industries, South Korea the 250m long British Merlin is an Aramax tanker owned BP Shipping. With a capacity of 115,000 tonnes of crude oil or fuel oil she is one of the largest merchant vessels at the review.

Aframax tankers are usually between 80,000 and 120,000 deadweight tons, designed to serve

British Merlin

RRS James Clark Ross

different trade routes and generally engage in both medium and short-haul trades carrying crude oil. The shallower draft and shorter length of these tankers enable them to enter a greater number of ports than the larger tankers at sea today

RRS James Clark Ross

Operated by the British Antarctic Survey, the Royal Research Ship (RRS) James Clark Ross is one of the most advanced oceanographic research vessels in the World. Large deck areas facilitate the deployment of a wide range of sampling gear and equipment for biological and geophysical studies. For the latter, there is a compressor bank to power a large seismic air gun array. She has 400 m2 of laboratory space. The vessel is equipped with modern instrumentation for continuous monitoring at sea and is designed to have an extremely low noise output to enable sensitive underwater acoustic equipment to operate effectively.

The ship can be driven at a steady two knots through level sea ice one metre thick. To assist passage through heavy pack ice a compressed air system rolls the ship and prevents the ice from squeezing the hull.

The James Clark Ross has just completed a successful season in Antarctica and two further scientific cruises on her voyage back to the UK. The first was surveying the sea floor around the island of Montserrat, West Indies in collaboration with the University of Bristol, British Geological Survey, Institut de Physique du Globe de Paris, France and Duke University, USA. The second was recovering a mooring deployed by the Institute of Marine Research, Norway.

She has been at Portland discharging Antarctic cargo and undergoing routine maintenance. Following the Fleet Review and IFOS, she will be dry docked in Portsmouth for her annual refit. She then has scientific cruises in the Arctic before the Antarctic season begins.

THV Patricia

THV Patricia is the flagship of the Trinity House fleet. Her normal duties involve maintenance of navigational buoys, attendance and refuelling of offshore lighthouses and dealing with emergencies, including wrecks. She is fitted with special towing winches, sufficient to pull a fairly large ship away from a dangerous situation as well as providing a routine capabil-

THV Patricia

ity for moving light ships to and from their stations. She has a 20 tonne speed crane capable of
lifting the largest navigational buoys. There is
also a flightdeck aft.

She is usually based at Harwich on the East
Coast but can regularly be seen at other ports
around the UK.

Although a working ship, this 2,500 ton vessel
can carry individual fare paying passengers or
corporate groups.

As flagship of the Trinity House fleet Patricia is

the only vessel allowed to prodceed the Royal
Yacht when the monarch is embarked.

MV Pharos

Operated by the Northern Lighthouse Board the
1,986 ton MV Pharos was built in 1993 as a
multi-purpose lighthouse tender. The ship has a
helicopter deck with fire protection and fixed
refuelling facilities, two cargo-holds and a main
crane capable of lifting any of the buoys around

MV Pharos

Queen Elizabeth 2

the coasts of Britain.

The Board is responsible for navigational aids around the coasts of Scotland and the Isle of Man. This area covers half the waters and coastline of the United Kingdom, together with the majority of offshore manned oil installations. The area is subject to severe weather conditions for many months of the year. The approximate length of this coastline is 6,214 miles (10,000km) a land area of 30,405sq miles (77,700 sq km) and 790 islands.

The ship itself carries out all types of work, from buoy maintenance and cargo-carrying in support of capital projects to the specialised Annual Inspection, Maintenance and Storage trips round the Board's lighthouses.

Queen Elizabeth 2

The Queen Elizabeth 2, or QE2 as she is commonly known was the flagship of the Cunard Line for over 30 years. She made her maiden voyage in 1969 and is one of the last great Transatlantic liners. At 70,327 tons and 963 feet long with a top speed of 32.5 knots she is also one of the largest and fastest passenger vessels afloat.

In 1982 the QE2 was requisitioned for the Falklands War as a troop transport, following in the footsteps of her famous forbear which carried out similar duties throughout the Second World War . On 12 May 1982 she set sail for St Georgia with 3000 troops aboard. She arrived safely back in Southampton on 11 June 1982.

Her current 4 day cruise saw her leave Southampton on 25 June for calls at St Peter Port, Guernsey and St Malo, France. Following the Fleet Review she will return to Southampton on the morning of 29 June.

Silver Cloud

Operated by Silversea Cruises and registered in the Bahamas, this 16,800 ton cruise ship was built in 1994.

She is currently on a 9 night European cruise

Silver Cloud

which started on 26 June at Honfleur, stopping at St Malo the following day before attending the Fleet Review. Her itinerary then takes her to Antwerp, Amsterdam, Hamburg and Ronne in Denmark via the Kiel Canal before ending on 5 July at Copenhagen.

CS Sovereign

CS Sovereign is a multi-role vessel capable of undertaking both subsea cable maintenance and installation projects. Her open deck enables her to deploy a variety of remotely operated vehicles and currently on board is the Atlas 1 ROV.

CS Sovereign

HM Customs Cutter Vigilant

DAVE CULLEN

Atlas is a powerful, state of the art cable working ROV, designed for both cable maintenance and post lay and inspection roles. With 300kW of installed power they have substantial cable intervention and burial capability and a range down to 2,000m water depth.

CS Sovereign is stationed at Portland, on the south coast of the United Kingdom, and provides repair and maintenance services to submarine cable systems in the Atlantic Ocean. She has a storage capacity of some 2800 cubic metres and a load capacity of 6,200 tonnes.

During Trafalgar 200, she will be captained by John Tollady.

HMCS Vigilant

Commissioned in June 2003, Her Majesty's Customs Cutter Vigilant is one of several modern counter-smuggling vessels built at a cost of £4.5 million each. Her patrol area is off the South East of England and the crew are on 30 minute stand-by to intercept potential targets. They work in all weathers, 24 hours a day, 7 days a week.

FPV Norna

Although Britain's sea fisheries have been pro-

FPV Norna

SCOTTISH FISHERIES PROTECTION AGENCY

Leopardess

tected and controlled by the authority of Parliament for nearly 200 years, the Scottish Fisheries Protection Agency was only formed as an Executive Agency of government in 1991. The Agency is funded by the Scottish Executive and is headed by a Chief Executive, who is accountable to the Scottish Parliament. The introduction of the Agency meant that all aspects of enforcement - policy, operations, ships, aircraft and fishery offices around the coast - and their management were brought together into a single unified organisation.

The Agency's principal role is the enforcement of fisheries legislation and regulations in the seas around Scotland and in Scottish ports.

FPV Norna is one of four vessels and two aircraft operated by the SFPA. Launched in 1987 this 1,385 ton vessel is 65 metres long, with a top speed of 18 knots. She is operated by a crew of 17.

Leopardess

The States of Guernsey Sea Fisheries are responsible for enforcing domestic and European fisheries legislation within the 3 mile territorial waters of the Bailiwick (Guernsey, Alderney and Sark) and British Fisheries limits adjacent to Guernsey (3-12 mile limit). Key to this enforcement work is the Departments fisheries protection vessel Leopardess. She was built by the Dutch firm Damen shipyards and entered into service in 1997. She is an 18.5 metre aluminium craft fitted with twin Volvo diesel engines producing a total of 1100hp. She is capable of a top speed of 26 knots. Boarding parties are deployed using a 5.5 metre delta rigid inflatable launched and retrieved via a stern ramp. This inboard diesel (120hp Mercruiser) powered vessel named 'Puma' was delivered in March 2003 replacing a Humber 5.8m outboard powered RIB of the same name.

Sea Vigil

Sea Vigil is a small 55 tonnes research vessel operated by the Environment Agency and conducts environmental monitoring in UK Home Waters from the Humber to Penzance.
Built in 1991 at Bristol this vessel has a crew of eight and can remain at sea for two days.

Pride of Bristol

The Pride of Bristol Trust was formed following the disbandment of the Royal Naval Auxiliary Service in the defense cuts of 1994. Some members, who had been on active duty in the main branches of the services felt that their years of experience could be put to some use in the local community - thus the Pride of Bristol Trust was formed
With the help of the National Lottery, National Westminster Bank and other local companies, funds were raised and an ex-RN Training Vessel was purchased. Many members had served in similar vessels and were therefore experienced in all aspects of taking her to sea.

The organisation increased in size with new members from the Royal Navy, Royal Navy Reserves and Merchant Navy plus local Yacht masters and Instructors adding their skills.
In 1997 the Trust started to take Trainees to sea. they were divided into watch groups and worked alongside the volunteer crew members. Groups from such organisations as the Prince of Wales Trust, St Johns Cadets and Scouts spent weekends or weeks learning all of the basic skills of seamanship, coastal pilotage, ship handling, helmsmanship and safety at sea, plus the more important skills of cooperation with others and pride in personal achievement.
To learn more about the trust visit:
www.prideofbristol.org

Amazon Hope

Amazon Hope 2 is the second of two mercy ships converted for operating on the Amazon in South America. She is currently on a whistlestop tour around the UK before departing for the Amazon later this summer. This former Royal Navy Fleet Diving Tender (ex-

Amazon Hope

MY Leander

Ixworth) has recently undergone a major refit and conversion to a floating medical centre with operating theatre,dental surgery and pharmacy. The ship has been recommisioned by the Princess Royal. The original Amazon Hope (ex-Milford) has been helping to provide a healthcare system for up to 100,000 people in remote communities in Peruvian Amazon since arriving in 2001.

By touring the UK the aim is to share the vision for the work; provide news of volunteering opportunities; and increase financial support.

Full details can be found at the website: www.vinetrust.org.uk

MY Leander

MY Leander is owned by Captain Sir Donald Gosling KCVO Kt RNR, President of the White Ensign Association. Sir Donald, who was co-founder of National Car Parks, took delivery of vessel from Peene Werft, Germany in 1992.

She is of 1,930 gross tonnage with a hull of steel construction and an aluminium superstructure. At 75 metres long with a helicopter deck

certified for 5 tonnes, she has a cruising range of 8000nm at 14.5 knots and a maximum speed of 18.5 knots. Leander is available for charter (reputably at in excess of £40,000 a day) in the Mediterranean or Caribbean. She has two master suites, three double guest suites, five twin guest cabins with bathrooms, a pool, a gym and a range of tenders, boats, wet bikes and jetskis. She has a crew of 24.

RAF SPT 206

A 37.5 ft Mk1 Seaplane Tender SPT 206 was ordered in May 1931 and commissioned into RAF service in March 1932.

She was discovered in Gweek, Cornwall in 1990 in a seriously dilapidated and almost unrecognisable state due to a series of modifications, which were part complete and out of keeping with the original design. At that time the paint was removed from her bows revealing her original RAF markings. ST 206 was subsequently acquired by Phil Clabburn who completely rebuilt her, restoring the craft to her original Seaplane Tender condition. She was re-

launched at Hythe on 17 July 1993, and is thus the first of the Powerboat Restorations craft to have been restored.

In her present guise, she has twin Cummins diesels fitted and has had her hull glass sheathed, otherwise she appears as she would have done over 60 years ago. ST 206 now represents the British Military Powerboat Trust at numerous events and often accompanies HSL 102.

For further information on the preserved vessels in the British Military Powerboat Trust collection visit: www.bmpt.org.uk

Motor Torpedo Boat 102

MTB 102 was designed (under the designation Vosper Private Venture Boat) by Commander Peter Du Cane CBE, Managing Director of Vosper Ltd., in 1936. She was completed and launched in 1937, and ran trials on the Solent.

She was bought by the Admiralty and commissioned as MTB 102, becoming the first MTB of the modern era.

Her service career saw her off the beaches of Dunkirk for the evacuation of the British Expeditionary Force and later carried Winston Churchill and General Eisenhower on their review of the ships assembled on the south coast for the D-Day landings, thus seeing the desperate evacuation of troops from Europe and their determined return.

She was sold off at the end of the war and converted to a private motor cruiser, fitted with two Perkins P.6 Diesels and used around the North Sea.

Twenty years later she was resold, and during her conversion to a houseboat she was found by a Norfolk Scout Group in 1973 and in need of much attention.

Help came in the shape of Kelso Films who agreed to refurbish 102 as a WWII MTB for their 1976 film *The Eagle Has Landed* after which she was returned as a fully operational sea going vessel.

The MTB 102 Trust has now been set up to obtain major sponsorship and finance to keep this unique vessel operating for as long as possible.

For more information visit:
www.mtb102.com

HMS Medusa

NICK NEWNS

HMS Medusa

Medusa was laid down as Harbour Defence Motor Launch ML1387 at R A Newman & Sons of Poole Dorset on 27 July 1943 and launched on 20 October 1943. She was involved in convoy escort in the Western Approaches before joining the 149th HDML Flotilla at Portsmouth and taking part in a practise assault carried out by the Americans at Slapton Sands in Devon. As the D-day landings she arrived off Omaha beach the night before and stayed on station throughout as a navigational marker.

Post war Medusa was redesignated Fast Despatch Boat 76 before being allocated to London Division RNVR as HMS Thames. Subsequently she was renamed Seaward Defence Launch (SDML) 3516 and in 1953 became a survey vessel and was named HMS Medusa.

Medusa is powered by two Gardner 8L3 diesels and a Gardner 1L2 auxilliary. She is armed with two 20mm Oerlikon (originally one Oerlikon and a 3 Pounder), Two Vickers K

MARITIME PHOTOGRAPHIC

Tug Challenge

Tug Brocklebank

DAVE CULLEN

machine guns and eight depth charges.

In 1968 she was sold by the Navy thought to be fit only for scrap. Since then, in private ownership, she has been maintained in her original configuration. She is now owned by The Medusa Trust and is operated by volunteers from the Medusa Support Group. She is on the Core Collection of the National Historic Ships Committee and is normally berthed in Southampton.

Challenge

Challenge was the last steam tug to serve on the Thames, where she spent her entire working life. Her first owner was the Elliot Steam Tug Co Ltd. but she was subsequently owned by Dick & Page, Sun Tugs, and then London Tugs. At the time of Dunkirk she towed some of the Little Ships across the Channel to save fuel and herself rescued troops. She was lying, out of use, at Gravesend from about 1971. After long negotiations, she was purchased by the Taylor Woodrow Group for the collection of historic vessels in St Katherine's Dock. In 1977, all 192 plain tubes in the boiler (there are a further 102 stay tubes) were replaced and she is now oil fired. By 1993 she had deteriorated badly and would have been scrapped. Thanks to the gen-

erosity of Sun Tugs and the Port of Tilbury, Challenge was moved to Tilbury Docks and a charitable trust established to restore her.

Brocklebank

The tug Brocklebank is owned by the Merseyside Maritime Museum. She was built by WJ Yarwood at Northwich in 1965 for Alexander Towing on the River Mersey.

FV Jacinta

The Jacinta is a preserved 599 ton wet-fish stern-trawler. She was built in 1972 and is a great example of the fishing vessels that could often been seen operating from the distant water fishing ports around the UK. Throughout her career she sailed from Fleetwood, Lancashire and latterly from Hull, East Yorkshire.

The Jacinta has now been restored and put back in a sea going condition, albeit no longer in a fishing role, operating primarily as a museum ship and is open for visitors at her home port of Fleetwood, Lancashire in the UK. She is in a fully working condition and often visits other ports around Britain and is available for private charter.

PREVIOUS FLEET REVIEWS

For the historian the study of previous gatherings of warships makes fascinating reading. A full list is given below.

1346	20 June	King Edward III	Before sailing for war with France. More than 1000 ships assembled and sailed for France in July.
1415		King Henry V	Before sailing for war with France. The advantages of Portsmouth Harbour so pleased the King that he orderd the Round Tower at Old Portsmouth to be built in order to defend Portsmouth from attack from the sea.
1582		Queen Elizabeth I	(and Agincourt) no details known
1662	May	King Charles II	No details known
1693	16 February	William III	After 'La Hogue'. Vice Admiral Rooke was knighted onboard the Flagship.
1700	March	William III	Visit of Peter The Great, Czar of Muscovy. This Review was possibly the first one in British waters to include a mock battle.
1773	June	King George III	The King was accompanied by the First Lord of the Admiralty Lord Spencer. The ships he inspected were veterans of the Seven Years War. The Review included a cruise to Sandown Bay, Isle of Wight, led by the Royal Yacht.
1778	4 May	King George III	No details known
1781		King George III	No details known
1794	15 June	King George III	After the 'Glorious First of June'. The only authenticated record of a victorious Fleet being reviewed by the Sovereign immediately it returned to harbour after battle.
1814	25 June	King George III	To celebrate the Treaty of Paris. The Czar of Russia and the King of Prussia attended as guests of the Prince Regent. The last

			Review in which only sailing vessels took part.
1842	1 March	Queen Victoria	The Queen's First Review (of 17 she attended).
1844	30 May	Queen Victoria	Visit of King of Saxony.
1844	8 October	Queen Victoria	Visit of King of France. The King of France landed at Gosport on this occasion. The Review took place as a French Naval Squadron left in company with a British Squadron.
1845	23 June	Queen Victoria	Experimental Squadron. The Experimental Squadron was formed to test the speed and seaworthiness of different designs of ship by various designers. The Royal Yacht at this Review was the paddle vessel Victoria and Albert. One steam warship was present.
1853	11 August	Queen Victoria	First Review of Steamships. Both screw and paddle warships were included at this Review. The Review ended with a race between the steamships and three sailing vessels of the line.
1854	10 March	Queen Victoria	Baltic Fleet before war.
1856	23 April	Queen Victoria	After return from the Baltic. As the Review took place on St Georges Day, HMS Royal George was the Fleet Flagship.
1865	August	Queen Victoria	Visit of French Fleet.
1867	17 July	Queen Victoria	Visit of Sultan of Turkey and Viceroy of Egypt. First occasion all ships flew White Ensign. Bad weather ruined this Review.
1873	23 June	Queen Victoria	Visit of Shah of Persia.
1878	13 August	Queen Victoria	Review of Reserve Squadron.
1887	23 July	Queen Victoria	Golden Jubilee Review. First appearance of a submarine at a Review.

1889	5-6 August	Queen Victoria	Visit of Kaiser Wilhelm II. The Kaiser was accompanied by Admiral Von Tirpitz - the famous World War II battleship was named after him. The young Commanding Officer of Torpedo Boat 79 later became King George V.
1891	20 August	Queen Victoria	Visit of French Fleet.
1896	1 August	Queen Victoria	Visit of MP's and Li Hung Chang. Queen Victoria actually reviewed the Fleet from Osborne (Isle of Wight) as it passed en route to the anchorage.
1897	26 June	Queen Victoria	Diamond Jubilee Review. Queen Victoria was, in fact, too frail to attend and the Prince of Wales (later King Edward VII) deputized for her.
1899	5 August	Queen Victoria	Visit of German Squadron.
1902	16 August	King Edward VII	Coronation Review. The Review was delayed because of the King's ill-health.
1905	9 August	King Edward VII	Visit of French Fleet.
1907	3 August	King Edward VII	Review of Reconstituted Home Fleet.
1909	31 July	King Edward VII	Review of Home and Atlantic Fleets. The first Review at which battlecruisers appeared.
1911	24 June	King George V	Coronation Review.
1'912	7-11 May	King George V	Inspection at Weymouth.
1912	9 July	King George V	Review for Houses of Parliament. 'Aerial craft' appeared for the first time, one making an ascent from HMS London.
1914	16 July	King George V	Mobilisation Review.
1919	17-23 July	King George V	Naval Victory Review at Southend.
1924	26 July	King George V	Naval Fleet Review. An aircraft carrier was present for the first time.

The minelaying submarine Porpoise at the 1935 Silver Jubilee Review

DAVID JOHN WELLER COLLECTION

1935	16 July	King George V	Silver Jubilee Review of Home, Mediterranean and Reserve Fleets.
1937	20 May	King George VI	Coronation Review.
1944	May	King George VI	Inspection of 'D' Day Anchorage. A little publicised visit, over 800 ships were present, mostly small landing craft, minesweepers and auxiliary vessels.
1953	15 June	Queen Elizabeth II	Coronation Review.
1969	16 May	Queen Elizabeth II	Twentieth Anniversary of NATO. The first Review when RN ships were outnumbered by those of other Navies. Guided missile and helicopter carrying warships prominent.
1977	28 June	Queen Elizabeth II	Silver Jubilee Review.

The Battleship HMS Barham at the 1935 Fleet Review

The Battleship HMS Vanguard heads a line of aircraft carriers at the 1953 Coronation Review

WHAT SHIP IS THAT MUM?

Most (but not all) warships carry their identifying (pennant) numbers painted on their ships side. Here is a list to help you identify some of the ships you may see. Full details are included earlier in this publication.

01	Finnish	Minelayer		F85	UK	Frigate
20	Pakistani	Tanker		F87	UK	Frigate
54	US	Cruiser		F103	Spanish	Frigate
57	South Korean	Tanker		F219	German	Frigate
70	US	Aircraft Carrier		F222	Romanian	Frigate
101	Japanese	Destroyer		F229	UK	Frigate
150	Australian	Frigate		F233	UK	Frigate
153	Japanese	Destroyer		F234	UK	Frigate
185	Pakistani	Frigate		F235	UK	Frigate
273	Polish	Frigate		F236	UK	Frigate
336	Canadian	Frigate		F237	UK	Frigate
605	Russian	Destroyer		F245	Turkish	Frigate
611	Moroccan	Frigate		F331	Portugues	Frigate
975	South Korean	Destroyer		F452	Greek	Frigate
3508	Japanese	Training Ship		F911	Belgian	Frigate
A53	Latvian	Support Ship		H86	UK	Survey Ship
A110	UK	Tanker		H88	UK	Survey Ship
A135	UK	Aviation Training Ship		H130	UK	Survey Ship
A171	UK	Ice Patrol Ship		H131	UK	Survey Ship
A301	South African	Support Ship		L12	UK	Assault Ship
A320	Estonian	Frigate		L14	UK	Assault Ship
A387	UK	Stores Ship		L15	UK	Assault Ship
A388	UK	Stores Ship		L17	Danish	Support Ship
A390	UK	Tanker		L110	UK	Landing Craft
A607	French	Tanker		L111	UK	Landing Craft
A960	Belgian	Support Ship		L113	UK	Landing Craft
				L800	Dutch	Assault Ship
D62	Indian	Destroyer		L3004	UK	Landing Craft
D89	UK	Destroyer		L3005	UK	Landing Craft
D90	UK	Destroyer		L3505	UK	Landing Craft
D91	UK	Destroyer				
D95	UK	Destroyer		M29	UK	Minehunter
D96	UK	Destroyer		M30	UK	Minehunter
D108	UK	Destroyer		M31	UK	Minehunter
D615	French	Destroyer		M32	UK	Minehunter
				M34	UK	Minehunter
F80	UK	Frigate		M35	UK	Minehunter
F81	UK	Frigate		M37	UK	Minehunter
F83	UK	Frigate		M51	Lithuanian	Minehunter

M104	UK	Minehunter		P279	UK	Patrol Craft
M107	UK	Minehunter		P281	UK	Patrol Craft
M108	UK	Minehunter		P291	UK	Patrol Craft
M109	UK	Minehunter		P293	UK	Patrol Craft
M112	UK	Minehunter		P294	UK	Patrol Craft
M861	Dutch	Minehunter				
M923	Belgian	Minehunter		Q32	Omani	Frigate
M1066	German	Minehunter				
				R05	UK	Aircraft Carrier
P31	Irish	Patrol Craft		R06	UK	Aircraft Carrier
P164	UK	Patrol Craft		R11	Spanish	Aircraft Carrier
P165	UK	Patrol Craft		R70	French	Aircraft Carrier
P258	UK	Patrol Craft				
P264	UK	Patrol Craft		S523	Italian	Submarine
P274	UK	Patrol Craft		S606	French	Submarine
P275	UK	Patrol Craft